M r. Chairman, you have asked me in your recent letter to help you and your fellow members of the Congress understand the deficit and to share my thinking on two very important questions. Those questions are:

1. We are particularly interested in hearing your reaction to the growing dissatisfaction with the present tax system as evidenced by unprecedented non-compliance.

2. Your views for overhauling our current approach and, in particular, how your suggestions might aid the Congress in lowering the budget deficit.

THE
ULTIMATE SELF INTEREST

A Strategy for National Solvency

The National Dividend Plan
and
House Bill 2740

John H. Perry, Jr.

Mr. Perry was asked during congressional testimony in 1983 for his best thinking on our damaging tax policy and solutions to the deficit. Mr. Perry responded. The Congress is beginning to act on his ideas. It will amaze you how powerful simple ideas can be.

3

A FEW COMMENTS ON MR. PERRY'S PLAN

"A daring plan to preserve the free enterprise system and reverse the trend toward national bankruptcy brought on by yearly federal budget deficits has been developed and should be implemented. Congress won't accept the National Dividend Plan and members will not **until they get pressure from the grassroots.**"

>   Dr. Martin R. Gainsbrugh
>   Former Chief Economist
>   The Conference Board

"THE NATIONAL DIVIDEND PLAN is more complex than the idea of a balanced-budget amendment, which is inching its way to national consideration. Yet it holds the hope of achieving far more widely shared goals."

>   Thomas Gephardt, Associate Editor
>   *Cincinnati Enquirer*

"As deficits continue to mount, this would be a good time for Congress to seriously consider a revolutionary plan to refinance the country. Some profound economic minds that have studied the concept—have become converts."

>   Editorial
>   *The Sacramento Union*

"I can't tell you how much I admire your steadfastness. The compelling logic of your case (and the interesting trade-offs you've developed). Too bad there aren't more great Americans like you to carry the ball."

>   William E. Simon
>   Former Secretary of the Treasury

"I believe this proposed legislation has a great deal of merit, and I hope that the House Ways and Means Committee will consider it carefully in the weeks ahead."

Howard H. Baker, Jr.
United States Senate

"It's a great idea."

Stanley J. Modic, Editor
Industry Week

"The logic is irresistible, and presents our lawmakers with a plausible structure for a truly **popular** economy."

Editorial
The Patriot-News Co.
Harrisburg, Pennsylvania

"I want to assure you of my continuing strong support for this legislation, and of my efforts to see that it does receive favorable action."

Guy Vander Jagt
Member of Congress

"I think your success to date is evidence of your devotion to the issue and we will watch with interest action on this legislation over the next several months."

Donald L. Calvin
Executive Vice President
New York Stock Exchange

"As a co-sponsor of the National Dividend Act, I assure you that I will continue to urge my colleagues to consider the merits of this legislation."

Carrol A. Campbell, Jr.
Member of Congress

FOREWORD

This book was written to save money — yours — and to present a simple, effective and proven plan to restore financial security for all of us as American citizens. The two objectives go hand in hand.

Although the issues discussed concern national economic policy, I hope you will find this book to be about you: Your financial future and how this is affected by our approach as a nation in dealing with our collective fiscal efforts and obligations. As with most major issues, I am convinced, an informed public leads the way to resolution. I hope this book contributes to that process.

A number of economists and policy leaders have reviewed, tested and now support the five steps to financial security presented in the following pages. I believe the real judge, however, will be you — the reader, taxpayer and voter — and I encourage you to give these steps your closest scrutiny.

I believe the time has finally arrived for the National Dividend Plan. It will immeasurably improve the financial strength of the United States and each of her citizens. It is, then, to the cause of a vibrant future for our country and for each of you that this book is dedicated.

John H. Perry, Jr.
Riviera Beach, Florida
September, 1987

CONTENTS

"SOLUTION OF THE DEFICIT PLAGUE PROVIDES OUR NATIONAL ELECTED OFFICIALS A CHANCE TO BE THE ECONOMIC STATESMEN OF THIS CENTURY."

—JOHN H. PERRY, JR.

INTRODUCTION

By Michael Novak

John Perry is a very creative guy.

Everybody else **says** something should be done about the deficit, **says** something should be done to help the poor, **says** something should be done to give the people a share in the ownership of corporations, **says** something should be done about making U.S. business innovative and future-oriented again.

John Perry has **done** something about it.

He has done the hardest and the most essential thing. He has come up with a NEW IDEA.

The idea itself — the National Dividend Plan (NDP) — is essentially simple. But there are so many things it does, explaining it has to proceed by steps. In addition, Washington's favorite rebuttal to any new idea is: "Can't be done." So, at each step, one has to pause to swat at objections as at mosquitoes. Good ideas need short books: therefore, this one.

The most important thing NDP offers is **hope.** [In March 1984, thirty-two Congressmen from both sides of the aisle and all political tendencies embodied NDP in a proposed new bill, H.R. 5085*. The idea is practical as well as visionary. Skeptics keep coming over.]

What I like best about H.R. 5085* is that it offers every citizen who votes an annual dividend from corporate profits. It gives everyone a stake in how well big business does each year. It adds a financial incentive to civic duty. All you need to do to claim your annual dividend is register to vote. Incentives are a lot better than sanctions, which some nations impose to insure larger turnouts than ours on election day. Incentives are the American Way.

* Reintroduced in the 100th Congress as H.R. 2740

NDP is good for citizenship. It's good for business, tying business success to broadly distributed benefits. And it's good for the poor — the NDP would lift a considerable number of families with two or more voters out of poverty.

But the kicker is what the NDP does to deficits. Each year, all taxes from corporate profits (frozen at a predictable level of 46 percent*) would go into a national trust fund. This fund would be used, first, to pay off the deficit, if any. After that, such taxes on corporate profits would be paid in equal dividends to every registered voter. The Plan would be phased in over five years, twenty percent of corporate profit taxes at a time.

During these five years, federal spending would be frozen. Year by year, deficits would be paid off. In four years, Mr. Perry's experts calculate, annual dividends would begin to go to voters.

As matters now stand, most of those unregistered to vote are poor, mostly whites but, in disproportionately high numbers, blacks, Hispanics and others. The NDP gives everyone a financial incentive to register and vote. It also gives the poor a big step up out of poverty — up to $1,000 per year per registered voter.

The following pages lay out the plan in clear and easy steps. You will see why one skeptic after another has been won over to it. A period of low inflation is an ideal time to launch this plan. President Reagan supported it; also Congressmen as diverse as Parren Mitchell (D) Maryland and Newt Gingrich (R) Georgia and many others. It is a brilliant, long-range political solution to an economic problem — so philosophically sound, practical, and fair that readers are likely to ask: "Why wasn't it enacted decades ago?"

If you don't believe in good ideas, if you are naturally skeptical, and if you think the above description is too good to be true — put your skepticism to the test. Read on.

* H. R. 2740 reflects the revised corporate tax rate of 34 percent

Chapter One

DEFICIT SPENDING

Almost every American today has, at one time or another, lived beyond his or her means. The temptations in modern society are great to spend now and worry about it later. We are coaxed by advertisements to "simply charge it." We are lured to purchases with "no payments for a month" and "easy terms."

For the average American, however, such an adventure in the use of credit is self-limiting. Eventually the bills must be paid and the cost is reduced consumption in the future. State and local governments also face a budget constraint on deficit spending. However, the federal government has a unique monopoly right to the creation of money. This allows it to escape the normal fiscal discipline of borrowing limits that are imposed on its citizens and states.

Government finance wasn't always this way. Since 1960, however, we have avoided deficits in only one year, 1969, and have seen the deficits accelerate dramatically as a percentage of Gross National Product (GNP). The moral and institutional barriers to deficit spending simply have broken down.

The prolificacy of federal spending has been reflected recently in the behavior of the American public as its savings rate has fallen to historically low levels. It is beyond argument that our government has led the massive infusion of the "buy now — pay later" mentality that is manifested in low personal savings, low domestic investment from U.S. sources, as well as the budget deficits. With increasing foreign capital the one consistent source of investment funds in the U.S., we are becoming the world's most-developed large debtor.

THE ULTIMATE SELF INTEREST

We face, literally, the loss of control over our economic destiny.

In recent periods of high inflation there was an individual incentive to buy on credit in order to avoid price increases. Even as inflation has abated, this binge of consumption has continued, fueled in large part by the level of stimulus provided by federal deficits. The resulting trade imbalance has become intolerable as well.

Today, our government is spending nearly $157 billion more annually than it receives in revenues. Our national debt is now approaching $2.4 trillion. It is costing us more than $190 billion each year in interest on the public debt. When we obtain the figure for net interest outlays of the federal government by making adjustments for the interest received by the government for on-budget and off-budget dedicated trust funds, as well as other interest, we still have a net outlay of over $136 billion per year. Even if the unrealistically low net interest figure is used, the federal debt is costing us an immense amount.

Costing "us?" That's right, 240 million Americans bear both the direct cost of taxation that services the federal debt and the lost output of the private sector that was displaced by government deficit spending. In summary, the numbers are discouraging.

THROUGH OUR FEDERAL GOVERNMENT, WE

- SPEND $157 billion MORE ANNUALLY than our revenue

- HAVE DEBTS of $2.4 trillion

- PAY MORE THAN $190 billion in INTEREST EACH YEAR on the PUBLIC DEBT

Numbers of this magnitude require comparison in order to grasp their full meaning. A billion is, in an accounting sense, just a million with an additional three zeroes. However, the late Senator Everett Dirksen might have reminded us that we are talking about real money.

The governmental spending spree in 1986 pushed the deficit to five percent of GNP, a significant share of the productive power of the economy and an unparalleled occurrence since World War II. This is more than triple the historical average of 1.5 percent over the period of 1960 to 1980.

This year marked the first time that a large deficit has persisted into the fifth consecutive year of an economic expansion. In 1988, we are expected to enter a record sixth straight year of economic recovery and the deficit is expected to increase over that in 1987. If we are unable to balance the federal budget at a time of unprecedented economic growth, then we will face a real emergency if a recession occurs in the future.

For our government, one billion dollars lasts less than nine hours. In fact, from the time you get up tomorrow morning until the time you go to bed again, our government will spend almost one-half billion dollars more than it receives in taxes and revenues. It will have to borrow this money, adding even more to our national debt.

This is money that our children will have to pay for in terms of the lost availability of real resources in the future, and in the lost autonomy over their financial future that results from our use of foreign capital to finance huge deficits.

Full realization of the magnitude of this overspending is shocking when we remember that we are in debt by more than $2.4 trillion. An increasingly unacceptable amount of this debt is owed abroad. We no longer can put off facing up to the problem, as we have in the past, by simply saying that we owe it to ourselves. While we created it, the burden of a large portion of this debt will be borne by our

15

children and they will owe much of it to people outside of our country. This debt is roughly equal to more than a half-year of output of GNP for our country. We must try to think through this almost incomprehensible number, because it will affect economic opportunities for many decades to come.

We will never be able to put our national finances in order if we continue such deficit spending and thus compound the problem. If current trends continue, our staggering $2.4 trillion debt will double in less than 10 years. Now, that is shocking!

How did we get into this critical situation? Simply put, by using a philosophy of stimulating the economy through solely "demand-side" economics. We took on more federal programs than we could afford. The motives and goals of these programs were sincere and well-intentioned, but the fact is that even the best programs may have some features built into them that create costly and destructive distortions in the economy. Taken in total, the excess of programs over available sources of funding has resulted in an unprecedented accumulated deficit that threatens future growth.

One of the side effects of too much government spending is rampant inflation, the kind we experienced in the late 1970's. By 1981, our government economists switched from "demand-side" economics to "supply-side" economics to reduce and control inflation and increase growth. The reduction of inflation, however, slowed the automatic growth of taxes that increased federal revenues, while spending continued to increase rapidly. This aggravated already serious budget deficits.

Add to this recent increases in military spending and the indexing of welfare and Social Security and the result is federal deficits that are fully out of control.

All of us would like to think that our lives are on a steady growth pattern. We want to be better off tomorrow than we are today. The facts, however, point in the opposite direction. The huge trade deficit, linked to the budget deficit, and the subsequent plunge in the value of the dollar have resulted in a tremendous decrease in the purchasing power of American incomes on world markets.

In addition, deficits are displacing available money to lend for both consumer and business needs. This threatens to limit the growth of income in the future.

How would you feel if your bank could only finance 50 percent of the purchase price of your new car, requiring a 50 percent down payment by you? Or if your credit card limit was reduced, overnight, from $1,000 to $100 by the Japanese investor who owned your bank? Consider if the only way you could purchase a new home was with a 40 percent down payment, a condition not uncommon to other countries. How effective would the United States be in a world where its financial actions were curtailed to a similar degree by a tremendous foreign debt and the ensuing restrictions placed on it by other governments and foreign banks, investors and corporations?

The danger of such a situation is real and present and it is linked almost exclusively to our huge national debt created by continuing and growing annual budget deficits.

Economists use the term "capital formation" as a convenient way of saying that the money individuals, businesses and state and local governments borrow is most often invested in productive capacity. The money comes from our savings accounts, the interest deposits of businesses, and pension funds, among other sources. The federal government spends borrowed money on real goods and services or passes it on to others in the form of transfer payments and it is spent. As a result, private sector job-creating activity is displaced, and growth is thereby retarded.

With every increase in the national debt (the borrowing done by our government), the amount of money available to lend to the rest of us decreases almost proportionally.

The evidence suggests that this is happening right now. Our

current budget deficits are likely to stay above the level of $100 billion for the next decade unless strong action is taken. These deficits will remain above four percent of our GNP. Compare that four percent figure to the fact that total net savings of the private sector — personal, business and pension funds — have averaged only seven percent of our GNP for the last 25 years. Continuing high deficits relentlessly eat away most of the net domestic savings available in the country.

If our government is using most of the available money to finance debt for its budget, where will the money come from to invest in new businesses that provide jobs? How will new factories and equipment be financed? How will we be able to buy a new car or home? Currently, a significant portion of funds demanded by the government and funds necessary for business investment are coming from Japan and Europe. This increasing foreign ownership of U.S. debts means that much of the source of future debt payments and control over financial decisions will be outside the United States.

What is the source of all this debt that is costing us more than $190 billion each year in interest alone, usurping our savings and slowing business growth? The source is our own elected federal government and the causes are policies that have allowed the acceleration of "budget-busting" spending.

The blame cannot be placed on any one President, Congress or political party. There's plenty of blame to spread around for the mismanagement of our tax money and we must accept some of it ourselves. We all request — often demand — expenditures from our government without considering the cost we will pay. The separation of spending decisions from the necessary financing always has been part of the political process. After all, since 1960 we have had only one year with a federal budget surplus.

In recent years, however, the problem has become acute as the deficits became an increasingly large share of GNP. Although the

Gramm-Rudman-Hollings initiative sought to regain fiscal discipline with a "gentlemen's agreement," it lacked sufficient incentives for individual legislators to make the extremely difficult reductions in planned spending that the law required. Unfortunately, with this lack of incentives coupled to a watering-down of the automatic expenditure reduction feature of the law, Gramm-Rudman-Hollings has slowed runaway deficit spending only slightly. As a result, current deficits are barely under the recent ones equal to five percent of our country's output.

If we are to have any hope of solving the economic crisis confronting us, we must examine those political and societal pressures within our system that cause runaway spending. We must find positive ways to restructure incentives and reduce deficits.

Some of the programs have good intentions that we simply don't have enough money to pay for. We continue to borrow to support $150 billion deficits each year and accumulate trillion dollar debts. We continue to finance current benefits at the expense of providing adequately for our future well-being. As a result, a heavy burden continues to fall on our families and future generations. We must choose a different road.

Consider some of the largest parts of the debt problem. Medicare is a meaningful program that had broad support when it was created. It provides many useful and essential benefits. Originally Medicare was estimated to cost $4 billion in 1980 but actually cost $32 billion. In 1986, the cost had soared to over $70 billion, more than double that of 1980. Even with recent efforts to contain these costs, the estimated budget for Medicare will increase by nearly $34 billion over the next five years.

Social Security exceeded the $100 billion budget level in 1979 after more than four decades of existence. By the end of 1987, only eight years later, that figure will have more than doubled to $208 billion. The current known, long-term liability for Social Security approaches $5 trillion.

THE ULTIMATE SELF INTEREST

The long-term liability for federal civil service and military pensions exceeds another trillion dollars. It appears that it is impossible to reduce the overly-large growth in federal pensions. Outlays for federal employee retirement and disability payments have grown to more than $43 billion in 1987.

The list seems endless. Each program appears harmless on an individual basis. However, they add up to a national debt that threatens the stability and growth of the United States and the free world.

LET'S FACE THE FACTS

• As a nation, we live far beyond our means

• We have amassed a national debt beyond comprehension

• We are adding to this debt every day

• Our standard of living is standing still

• Government borrowing could prevent your borrowing

• All borrowing is increasingly supplied by foreign countries

• Hard choices must be made on our social programs

Chapter Two

SEARCHING FOR SOLUTIONS

We didn't reach our current financial crisis because of a lack of warning. We have produced a surplus in our national budget only once since 1960 and we should be quite familiar with deficits.

In a real sense we reached this point because the "we" became "them." In essence, our government became so big, moved so fast, seemed so complicated that we — you and I and most other Americans — withdrew from the process. We abdicated our vitally important responsibilities as citizens, as taxpayers. Most of us paid our taxes, and then most of us looked the other way.

It is individually that we must begin the search for solutions. When we realize the impact and magnitude of our national financial situation, concern and concentration will become possible and we can begin to believe we can do something about it. The problem will receive the attention needed to achieve a solution.

The question here is: If we have developed a plan to correct the problem, can we make it happen? Of course the answer is a simple, but emphatic: " Yes."

Most of us have grown accustomed to the mirage that Washington is government and that Washington exists mainly on the evening news. Runaway deficits, however, bring the impact of misguided governmental policy into our daily economic life.

Sure, our federal government is big. It's huge. Like our national debt, it can sometimes seem incomprehensible. But you can put your finger on it. If you have your last pay stub, find the column for the Federal Insurance Contributions Act (FICA) deduction and you've identified part of the problem. All programs have grown to be part of the problem.

Now comes the decision we as a nation must make: Are we willing to take responsibility, develop a plan of action, make the tough choices, implement the Plan, and stick to it? If we are not, then the future holds little hope.

Congress has the power to control federal spending. We have the power — in fact, the obligation — to control Congress, and our administrative agencies, our President, our state and local governments. "We the People" connotes responsibilities as well as privileges and rights. The citizen remains the ultimate check on irresponsible government actions.

The current economic strategies all accept as a given, "the current state of affairs," and hence do not provide direction. A review of what is being offered in the way of proposed solutions to our staggering deficits reveals that such solutions are incomplete. They fail to provide the political incentives necessary to insure success.

No conceivably obtainable rate of growth can keep up with the increase of government programs in the current, uncontrolled environment of government growth. No amount of increases in the various forms of taxes on citizens and businesses can assure a balanced budget in the face of unrestrained growth of spending, engineered by well-organized special interests.

The record is clear on the fate of countries that have allowed national government activity to become the primary factor in the economy, whether the budget was balanced or not. They do not grow, they do not innovate, and they do not provide adequate employment opportunities for their citizens. I do not believe that America is ready to throw in the towel to slow growth and overwhelming government at a time when Asia, Africa, Eastern and Western Europe and even the Soviet Union are moving decisively in the other direction. Our current situation can lead to such an unhappy situation, simply by our failure to act decisively.

Currently, a non-comprehensive solution that fails to fundamentally restructure the intense political incentives for big spending can not hope to deal with the complexities of our financial, economic and political realities. Also, budget cuts that focus exclusively on those federal expenditures that are considered "discretionary" can not hope to succeed. There would be enormous interest group pressure to have their pet programs included in the non-discretionary category. As a result, the complete elimination of the remaining expenditures would not likely eliminate the deficit. A freeze in spending, in the absence of any corresponding political benefits and specific future incentives could not be expected to hold together for any length of time. This has been the lesson of the Gramm-Rudman-Hollings effort.

Knowing that incomplete approaches were being considered in Washington, thus delaying a lasting solution, strengthened my resolve to get involved in this process. The National Dividend Plan was heard clearly by those who were disturbed that something was fundamentally wrong with what historically has been proposed to solve the deficit problem.

You find nowhere in previous proposals the element of political incentives to change the pressures that we place on our elected officials to over-spend. You find no complete answers to our capital formation crisis. There are no hints — much less guarantees — of secure control of government spending and the size of government in the future.

We can do better.

First, we need a plan. The partial, quick fix approach has not worked in the past, and it will not work in the future as political and economic pressure intensifies. We need a simple but comprehensive plan, one that includes not only sound remedies, but also assumes a solid national character. We need a plan that will restore our belief in our political process and our confidence in our free enterprise system. If we are going to devote our efforts, let's do it right.

Chapter Three

THE NATIONAL DIVIDEND PLAN

Five Steps to Financial Security

With the exception of our mammoth budget deficits and the related problems in our trade balance, little of the recent economic news is bad. The Plan outlined and explained here can lead us out of the economic and political morass of budget deficits and into a future with real gain for all Americans. It is not a new proposition. Rather, it is a result of a simple rejection of the basic erroneous beliefs that underpin the most vocal current economic and political thinking. Over the last decade, this plan has been studied and scrutinized in every detail by intelligent people, including prominent economic leaders and many at universities. And its credibility as a common-sense solution to the potential disaster confronting our nation has grown steadily.

The proposal is the National Dividend Plan. It is a comprehensive plan for the comprehensive budget problem.

The National Dividend Plan is a complete proposal to revitalize the most powerful economic machine in history, the American Economy, and to allow all American citizens to participate and benefit from this success. The Plan accomplishes this by instituting five basic reforms that will encourage participation in the private sector and assure a balanced federal budget.

Best described as a combination of fiscal and tax policies designed to enhance economic growth, reduce unemployment and control inflation, the National Dividend Plan provides a new way of conducting United States fiscal policy. It creates incentives for our representatives to respond to the overall public interest and to conduct our national financial affairs on a sounder basis.

Of particular importance, the National Dividend Plan creates incentives for cooperation between American business, the backbone of our economy, and American citizens, the political backbone of our democracy. Under the Plan we not only promote and encourage the profitable expansion of the American economy, we contribute to the health of our political institutions as well. With the National Dividend Plan, we overcome the current incentives to ask our elected representatives for more than they can possibly deliver and reduce the risks to the political and economic fabric of our society.

STEP ONE

A TEMPORARY MORATORIUM ON MAJOR FEDERAL EXPENDITURE PROGRAMS IS IMPOSED

This is essential to the Plan, and it is necessary to bring our federal budget under control again. Step One applies not just to programs of the federal budget that we might individually dislike but to the total spending package. Sacrifices will have to be made by everyone and every group involved in federal spending: national defense, civil service pensions, welfare and assistance programs, business and agricultural programs.

An across-the-board budget freeze, with every group sharing the impact, is the only way to seize control of runaway spending. The available evidence, discussed in Chapter Four, suggests that such a temporary moratorium would not have to last more than two, or at the most, three years in order to take our federal budget into a surplus condition.

THE NATIONAL DIVIDEND PLAN

STEP TWO

CREATE NATIONAL DIVIDEND TRUST FUND

The central innovation of the Plan is the creation of the National Dividend Trust Fund. After achievement of a federal budget surplus, the Fund would build by 20 percent of corporate tax revenues each year for five years until all corporate taxes were placed in the Fund.

This is a Fund for Americans, and from it we (1) balance our national budget (see Step Five) and (2) become directly involved in both our national budget process and our national productivity. After we balance the budget, all trust funds will be distributed, in quarterly dividends, to all registered voters in the United States. Moreover, by distributing dividends through our banking system with the incentive of interest free deposits for short periods, we utilize our enterprise system and avoid any new government bureaucracy and cost.

A plan, a trust fund, a balanced budget, a dividend for Americans. This is a lot to expect, but our comprehensive plan delivers, and the benefits speak for themselves.

STEP THREE

CAP CORPORATE TAXES AT 34 PERCENT

Currently, the maximum corporate tax rate is 34 percent. Step Three of our plan would simply lock in this level to avoid the temptation and inevitable political pressures to increase the corporate tax rate to achieve larger dividends after the budget is balanced. This step assures that we do not strangle the "golden goose" that creates our prosperity and provides the National Dividend.

THE ULTIMATE SELF INTEREST

Since our plan encourages us to promote and share in the success of our American business economy, it is clearly not in our best interests to discourage business development through higher or unpredictable tax rates. Step Three avoids this and provides investors assurances that tax rates will not hamper the level of investments necessary to rekindle business growth.

Capping the corporate tax rate also enables business executives to plan capital outlays for expansion and new ventures without worrying about an unexpected increase in corporate income taxes. In other words, we want businessmen and women to make business decisions, not tax decisions. In effect, this step is merely an extension of the spirit that moved the recent bipartisan tax reform.

STEP FOUR

END DOUBLE TAX ON DIVIDENDS

Profits are the very nucleus of our American free enterprise system. Without real profits there can be no prosperity, no full employment, no advances in technology, no improvement in our competitive world trade position, no earned money to support government and, now, no National Dividend Trust Fund.

Corporations seek to earn profits. Based on these profits corporations pay taxes, and dividends to shareholders. And in that order. For these shareholders to face additional personal income taxes on the same money is a double tax and should be eliminated.

Step Four of our plan accomplishes this by making dividends received by individuals through both stock ownership and from the National Dividend Trust Fund exempt from any federal tax. This step has additional benefits, including encouraging savings and investments which spur capital formation. Step Four has the added bonus of simplifying the current Internal Revenue Code.

STEP FIVE

GET OUR FEDERAL BUDGET IN SURPLUS

Our objective throughout this plan has been to come to grips with our massive national debt and financial crisis. The first place to start is with our continuous budget deficits. Accordingly, our plan requires that the total funds in the National Dividend Trust Fund be reduced each year by the amount of any federal budget deficit. We must accomplish our objective before we reward ourselves with a dividend.

This feature of the Plan is called the Automatic Dividend Deduction (ADD) which gives every American voter a vested, self-interested reason to resist federal deficits. No balanced budget, no national dividend. This feature helps accomplish the important realignment of incentives to the individual citizen in our budgetary process. As we discuss in the next chapter, this surplus could be expected to materialize in as little as two and no more than three years under current economic conditions.

Recent research, based on 1986 figures and projections, shows that implementing our Plan would produce a budget surplus in less than three years. After that, it will be up to us to make sure that our elected leaders in Washington understand the difference between deficit spending and reelection.

I am convinced, as are a growing number of our national political leaders and economists, that the National Dividend Plan is the fiscally and politically feasible alternative around which we can build a grass-roots constituency that can regain control of this country's financial destiny before it's too late.

The National Dividend Plan is a carefully crafted plan, many years in development, that has been subjected to severe testing, refinement and analysis. Beyond being carefully designed to solve the problem, it is a plan that has been tested and proven feasible. The National Dividend Plan offers us five steps to financial security:

1. Freeze Federal Spending
2. Create National Dividend Trust Fund
3. Cap Corporate Taxes at 34 percent
4. End Double Tax on Dividends
5. Get Our Federal Budget in Surplus

Through each step we regain control of our financial destiny, reinvolve ourselves in the political process, promote and share in the real productivity of our economy, balance our budget and provide the political incentives to keep it that way.

Now that's progress!

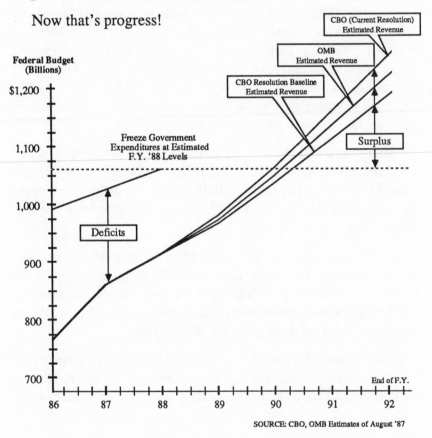

SOURCE: CBO, OMB Estimates of August '87

Chapter Four

EVIDENCE AND ANSWERS FOR SKEPTICS

The components of the National Dividend Plan are designed to work in a comprehensive way. As a result, there is an interactive synergy in the complete plan. The source of these benefits is not magic. Rather it is the common sense of structuring individual economic incentives in a rational way to encourage productive rather than destructive efforts in our economy and society.

Each of the components has been found to be beneficial as an individual change in our economy. The coordination of these changes produces significant improvement in the expected performance of the economy when estimated using macroeconomic simulations.

The budget freeze may seem to be the most politically ambitious part of the National Dividend Plan. How would politicians curry the favor of voters during a time when expenditures by the federal government are not increasing? However, at a time when deficits and public resentment of deficit spending are at an all time high, the expected time needed to solve the problem is relatively short and the potential political rewards are substantial. Solution of the deficit plague provides our national elected officials a chance to be the economic statesmen of this century. And the solution is much less difficult than it may at first appear.

Recent research by the prestigious Center for Study of Public Choice indicates that an across-the-board freeze of federal expenditures would need only about two and a half years to bring our excessive budget deficits into surplus. This is certainly a brief period to stop cold a problem that has developed over at least 30 years. A long-term political contribution of such historic proportions should capture the attention of our elected officials. Importantly, the tangible reward of the National Dividend Plan is an immediately attractive and understandable benefit to voters that offsets the short-term difficulty of a freeze.

The double taxation of dividends from corporate earnings, taxed once at the corporate level and again when the individual stockholder receives them, has long been known to hamper capital formation and economic growth. It promotes the retention of corporate earnings which results in bureaucracy, empire building and sluggish management within our corporations and, as a result, hampers our international competitiveness.

Even when income is retained by the corporation as a result of the double taxation of dividends, it is overtaxed. The problem of over taxation of corporate income is stated clearly in the Foreword of a study in 1986 by Dr. J. Gregory Ballentine for the National Chamber Foundation of the Chamber of Commerce of the United States:

> Dr. Ballentine concludes that aggregate effective corporate tax rates for many years have been consistently too high. Investors pay taxes on their income at individual rates. In addition, through the corporation, investors pay taxes on undistributed profits, which are taxed at a higher aggregate rate than the one on personal income. Shareholders are penalized as a result of this tax on undistributed profits. The result is a distribution of resources away from investment in corporations and toward alternative types of investment, thus hampering economic growth.

In effect, there is a double tax on retained corporate earnings as well since individuals eventually will cash in their investment. In addition, a third "tax" of inefficiency is borne by investors when corporations retain excessive earnings because of the inequitable

32

tax treatment of dividends. Elimination of the double taxation of corporate dividends would improve the efficiency of U.S. corporations and promote growth. Also, individual citizens would exercise greater control over their personal assets.

It is not surprising that savings by individuals in this country are at an historical low in a tax structure abusive for investment. Elimination of the double taxation of corporate dividends as well as provision of a national dividend would be two large steps toward restoring the competitiveness of American industry.

Each independent pillar of the National Dividend Plan is a desirable improvement in the economic and political system. The interaction of incentives in the complete Plan results in total benefits greater than the summation of benefits resulting from the individual components. When the entire Plan is simulated in a macroeconomic model, the benefits for the economy are striking. Recent large growth in deficits makes more urgent the need for the Plan.

The Plan has been studied by many independent economists and research organizations over an extended period of time. In 1970, for example, Lionel D. Edie and Company, long one of America's most highly respected economic research firms, conducted a nine-month, in-depth study and attested to the Plan's feasibility. In its final report, this prestigious firm endorsed the National Dividend Plan.

Following this analysis, Dr. Martin Gainsbrugh, formerly Chief Economist and Senior Vice President of The Conference Board, devoted five years to the study of the Plan. In a nationally broadcast interview in 1976, Dr. Gainsbrugh announced: "I can now demonstrate to my own satisfaction, and to the satisfaction of a growing number of economists, that this Plan is economically feasible."

Additional testing of the Plan was conducted in early 1980 by Leon Kilbert, a noted economist and former Vice President of Chase Manhattan Bank Investor Management Corporation. Using official federal government budget estimates and statistics, he developed a theoretical model with the National Dividend Plan in effect as of October 1980.

His research found dramatic results: A budget surplus was achieved quickly and up to $300 billion was distributed to registered voters during the five-year phase-in period. Annual dividends per voter exceeded $800 tax free.

Later in 1980, Merrill Lynch Economics was commissioned to undertake an impact analysis of the National Dividend Plan using projections for 1981-1987. The study consisted of projecting the Plan into the Merrill Lynch Macro-Econometric Model and examining its effects on key economic variables. The Merrill Lynch "bottom line" on the study: "Enhanced real growth and reduced inflation emerge as the chief outcome of applying the provisions of the National Dividend Plan."

A state by state estimate of the economic impact of the program, prepared by Dr. Paul Taylor of the Fiscal Policy Council, appears in the Appendix. Using the latest available figures from the Federal Election Commission on registered voters and a conservative estimate of corporate profit levels, a state with 1.2 million registered voters could expect about $1 billion in direct payout to state voters with the National Dividend Plan in full operation. With a multiplier effect, this infusion could be expected to have a total economic impact of over $3 billion for the state and increase personal savings in the state by about $55 million. Clearly, we are talking about a significant contribution to state and local economies at the same time that our national budget crisis is being resolved.

The evidence that the plan will benefit our economy is overwhelmingly positive. We must now make sure that there are no obstacles to instituting the Plan. If it is to be implemented as national policy, we want first to make sure we understand the Plan's operation and believe that it can work.

The implementation of the Plan will not cause any shortfall in tax revenues. The contribution to the trust fund does not begin until a surplus budget is achieved. Federal revenues historically grow at about 10 percent each year. Twenty percent of corporate income tax collections set aside each year represents less than two percent of total government revenue. Consequently, a net increase in revenues of more than eight percent a year will be available to the government in each year of the phase-in period.

The voters will share the federal corporate income taxes collected annually by the U.S. Treasury. The tax rate would continue to be set by the Congress, but the National Dividend Plan sets an absolute ceiling of 34 percent. The Plan would, of course, allow the rate to be set downward over time to stimulate increases in corporate productivity. This would guarantee a maximal National Dividend paid from increased profits and economic growth.

One of the most appealing features of the Plan is its exact equality of treatment of all registered voters. Each will receive exactly the same amount of money in the distribution of the Plan's Trust Fund. This sets the Plan apart from most government programs which benefit only selected segments of the American population.

The Plan will require no new or increased taxes. It simply creates a more efficient set of incentives from taxes already being collected.

The National Dividend Plan will put earned, non-inflationary dollars where the people and the problems are, without regard to bureaucratic or political pressure. Transfer payments, on the other hand, distribute debt financed or tax-added, inflationary dollars under formulae developed by bureaucracy — often with more concern for political advantage than for the taxpayers' welfare. The National Dividend Plan avoids these types of problems because it does not require a big bureaucracy or complicated disbursement process.

With the National Dividend Plan in effect every registered voter will have an equal share in the achievements of our free enterprise system, as shown in its earnings, just as all Americans share in the privileges and responsibilities of citizenship. One important factor in the per capita distribution is that those who don't need the dividend to meet immediate expenses are likely to save and invest those funds and thus contribute to the further expansion, production and profits of our economy. This will create more jobs and more earnings for distribution in dividend payments. And since the source of the dividend, American industry, is well identified, a strong incentive to purchase American-made goods is created.

The Plan is likely to create additional jobs: (1) by providing a continuing source of new investment capital, thus encouraging expansion and modernization of existing plants, construction of new ones, research into and development of new products and industries, all of which require more employees; (2) by providing more incentive to work, since increased corporate earnings mean increased corporate tax collections and increased payments to voters; and (3) by providing more purchasing power for more American-made products.

The five-year phase-in period prevents chaotic disruption of the economy which is now so deeply intertwined with countless federal spending programs. This will permit the gradual increment of government income from economic growth to keep pace with corporate income tax collections being devoted to the National Dividend Plan. The Treasury Department, through its Internal Revenue Service, would simply continue to collect federal corporate income taxes as it does now. Distribution would be administered easily on the state and local levels using voter registration records which already are being maintained throughout the country.

The federally regulated banking system would handle the actual disbursement of funds. The Plan allows Congress and the state legislatures to decide how and which banks are selected. Almost every bank, however, will be willing and eager to participate in administering the distribution since the Plan calls for placing interest-free deposits with these banks for specified periods of time prior to their distribution.

The Plan's distribution on a per capita basis to persons registered to vote is the most equitable method. It also is the most economical administrative method because the distribution network already exists. The fact that the Plan might encourage more citizens to exercise their constitutional right to vote is an additional benefit. These features all ease the way for implementation of the Plan. Local officials will have a strong economic incentive to keep voter registration timely and accurate in order to assure that the greatest number of dividend checks are endorsed and cashed in the locality.

The Plan in no way disturbs the property rights of the shareholders. It merely distributes, in a different and more direct manner, tax funds that already are being collected. Moreover, corporate shareholders benefit directly from the Plan's provision to eliminate personal taxes on dividends.

The implementation of the Plan helps states and counties by injecting more real dollars into the economy at the local level. Revenues to the state and localities from sales and excise taxes would be greatly increased. In addition, even though there would be no federal tax on dividends, states could impose their own.

The National Dividend Plan is based squarely on the American free enterprise system. Dividends are from profits of American business that would normally go into the vast pot of federal revenue, a contribution for which corporations rarely receive adequate credit. No new bureaucracy is created. People are involved in the enhancement and growth of the private sector, not in creating excessive government. This is pure capitalism and is probably the only proposal on the horizon that offers a strong antidote to our current fiscal decay. Indeed, in the Plan, corporations will receive direct, tangible recognition from citizens for the wealth created through the linkage of the dividend.

The National Dividend Plan is simple and practical. I began to develop this plan in the 1940's when the fiscal discipline of the United States was more robust. Many others have contributed to improving the Plan over the years. The current fiscal morass clearly calls for decisive action. The issue now becomes informing the public about the Plan so we can get on with the business of implementing it.

Fortunately, for all of us, several actions have already taken place that enhance our prospects for success and allow us to focus our individual efforts. First, more than 30 dedicated Members of Congress have supported this Plan as cosponsors. This legislation (see Appendix) is gaining broad support in the Congress as more and more Representatives and Senators study the Plan and learn of their constituents' support for it.

Second, a national organization has been formed to promote enactment of H.R. 2740 and provide updated information on the Plan. This organization, Americans for the National Dividend Act (ANDA), is headquartered in the Washington, D.C. area and growing in strength daily.

Third, the good news is spreading throughout the country that there is, in fact, a bold and workable plan to resolve our national financial crisis. Through reading this book, public briefings and seminars, information from the Americans for the National Dividend Act and the media, Americans in every state are learning how the National Dividend Plan can restore their own financial security.

Now we must turn our enthusiasm into action, and I recommend a few simple steps we can all take to secure our future.

Chapter Five

GETTING STARTED: WHAT YOU CAN DO

Like all solid ideas, the National Dividend Plan will require broad public support to become national policy. Since we have taken responsibility for our financial crisis, we must now take responsible action to correct it.

Those actions lie within each of us and it is up to us to take the steps to make this plan a reality.

The length of the road to recovery will be determined by our individual commitment to implement the Plan.

STEP ONE: KNOW THE PLAN

I have purposely kept this discussion of our financial crisis and how the National Dividend Plan can solve it brief and to the point — so that you can read and learn the facts rapidly. Take the time, however, to fully understand the issues. Think it through. Analyze each facet of the Plan. Keep in close touch with the office of the Americans for the National Dividend Act.

Knowing the facts equips you for action. Every other step you take to help launch the Plan will require a thorough understanding of it. How extensive is our national debt? What are the current projections on this year's budget deficit? How did we get into such debt, and how do we get out? What does this mean to you, your children's future, your long-term financial security? Ask your Congressman and Senators for the current facts and express your support for the Plan.

THE ULTIMATE SELF INTEREST

STEP TWO: SHARE THE IDEA

Now that you have read the Plan — share it.

Explain the Plan to a friend and answer his or her questions. Can you think of tough questions? Can you find the answers within these pages? If not, write me or the Americans for the National Dividend Act (see Appendix) and get the answers.

STEP THREE: DEMAND ACTION

In the final analysis, only 536 of your fellow Americans decide your future financial security and whether it will be enhanced by the National Dividend Plan — 535 Congressmen and Senators and one President of the United States. Sooner or later these Americans will decide the merits of the National Dividend Plan, consider enactment of H.R. 2740, and determine the course of our financial future.

Will they make the correct decisions? Will they know how their constituents view these issues? Will your Congressman and Senators know how you feel?

Remember that we got into our financial crisis by abdicating our responsibilities as citizens and taxpayers. This time demand action. Write your Congressman. Write both of your Senators. Write the President. Make sure they know where you stand on the National Dividend Plan, that you want them to support H.R. 2740 and that you want to be kept informed of their action and support.

Information on how to write your Congressman and Senators can be found in the Appendix of this book. Let them hear from you.

STEP FOUR: STAY INFORMED

As support for the National Dividend Plan strengthens over the coming months, particularly with the expected action in Congress in 1988 and beyond, the pace of events involving the Plan will quicken. Since these actions could affect your future, you should stay informed.

WHAT YOU CAN DO

You can receive updated information from the Americans for the National Dividend Act. Keep an eye on the media — and the business and financial press, in particular — for news of developments on the Plan. Look for articles, stories and reports on our national budget process and our federal deficits. All of this information is about you and your financial future. Don't miss it.

What is happening with the National Dividend Plan? What is the status of H.R. 2740? Are your Congressman and Senators supporting it? By staying informed, you will know the answers. And you will know what further actions you might need to take.

STEP FIVE: STAY INVOLVED

Implementing the National Dividend Plan will take effort by all of us over a concentrated period of time. But it can be done. It must be done, because in large part our children's future depends on it.

Our patience should be equalled only by our determination. It is worth it.

We have the opportunity today to shape our future and control our destiny; to strengthen our already powerful American economy; to promote and share in the success of our dynamic free enterprise system; to stop mortgaging our children's future through outrageous budget deficits and start laying the base for their financial security.

Throughout these pages we have examined the critical national issues that so greatly determine our financial future. We have accepted responsibility for our current problems, developed a plan to correct them, and committed ourselves to implementing the Plan. It is, after all, in our ultimate self interest.

APPENDIX

100TH CONGRESS
1ST SESSION

H. R. 2740

To establish The National Dividend Plan by reforming the budget process, and by amending the Internal Revenue Code of 1986 to eliminate the double tax on dividends, to allocate corporate income tax revenues for payments to qualified registered voters, and for other purposes.

IN THE HOUSE OF REPRESENTATIVES

JUNE 23, 1987

Mr. ALEXANDER introduced the following bill; which was referred jointly to the Committees on Ways and Means and Rules

---

A BILL

To establish The National Dividend Plan by reforming the budget process, and by amending the Internal Revenue Code of 1986 to eliminate the double tax on dividends, to allocate corporate income tax revenues for payments to qualified registered voters, and for other purposes.

1   *Be it enacted by the Senate and House of Representa-*

2 *tives of the United States of America in Congress assembled,*

3   **SECTION 1. SHORT TITLE.**

4   This Act may be cited as the "National Dividend Act of

5   1987".

1 SEC. 2. NATIONAL DIVIDEND PAYMENT TO REGISTERED
2   VOTERS.

3   (a) PAYMENTS FOR DISBURSEMENTS TO REGISTERED
4 VOTERS OF EACH STATE.—

5   (1) IN GENERAL.—The Secretary shall pay during
6   each calendar year after the Base Year to the chief fi-
7   nancial officer of each State an amount equal to the
8   National Dividend Payment for the immediately pre-
9   ceding calendar year multiplied by the number (provid-
10   ed to the Secretary by such officer) of individuals who
11   are qualified registered voters of such State for such
12   preceding year.

13   (2) SEMIANNUAL INSTALLMENTS.—One-half of
14   the amount payable under paragraph (1) to the chief
15   financial officer of any State during the 3 calendar
16   years immediately following the Base Year shall be
17   paid to such officer at the beginning of the second and
18   fourth calendar quarters of such year.

19   (3) QUARTERLY INSTALLMENTS.—One-fourth of
20   the amount payable under paragraph (1) to the chief
21   financial officer of any State during any calendar year
22   subsequent to the third calendar year immediately fol-
23   lowing the Base Year shall be paid to such officer at
24   the beginning of each calendar quarter of such year.

1 (b) AMOUNT OF NATIONAL DIVIDEND PAYMENT.—
2 The National Dividend Payment for any calendar year shall
3 be an amount equal to—

4   (1) the excess of—

5   (A) the sum of—

6   (i) the aggregate amount transferred
7   under section 3(b)(3) to the National Divi-
8   dend Payment Trust Fund during the fiscal
9   year ending during such calendar year, plus

10   (ii) any interest credited during such
11   fiscal year to the Trust Fund under section
12   3(c)(2)(B)(iii),

13   over

14   (B) the sum of—

15   (i) the amount transferred out of the
16   Trust Fund during such fiscal year under
17   section 3(b)(4), plus

18   (ii) the deficit adjustment amount for
19   such fiscal year calculated pursuant to sec-
20   tion 6 of this Act,

21   divided by

22   (2) the number of individuals who are qualified
23 registered voters for such calendar year as determined
24 on the basis of reports submitted not later than No-
25 vember 30 of such calendar year by the chief financial

1   officer of each State to the Secretary (in such manner

2   as the Secretary may by regulations prescribe).

3   (c) METHOD OF DISBURSEMENTS TO QUALIFIED REG-

4   ISTERED VOTERS.—

5   (1) IN GENERAL.—The National Dividend Pay-

6   ment for any calendar year shall be paid to each quali-

7   fied registered voter of a State by an incorporated bank

8   which is selected (in accordance with paragraph (2)) for

9   such year by the chief financial officer of such State as

10 the disbursing agent of such State.

11   (2) SELECTION OF DISBURSING AGENT.—Any in-

12 corporated bank may be selected as the disbursing

13 agent of any State under paragraph (1) by the chief fi-

14 nancial officer of such State if—

15   (A) such bank is determined by such officer

16   to be operating within such State,

17   (B) such bank submits a sealed bid to such

18   officer in which such bank—

19   (i) specifies an amount which it agrees

20   to pay such State as consideration for each

21   year for which it pays National Dividend

22   Payments to qualified registered voters of

23   such State,

24   (ii) specifies procedures which it agrees

25   to follow in making such payments, and

1   (iii) agrees to limit the investment of

2   any funds received for the purpose of making

3   such payments to interest-bearing obligations

4   of the United States or to obligations guar-

5   anteed as to both principal and interest by

6   the United States,

7   and

8   (C) such officer approves such bid, taking

9   into account with respect to all such bids—

10   (i) the amount of such consideration,

11   (ii) any previous experience of such

12   bank in making such payments, and

13   (iii) the ability and reliability of such

14   bank to make such payments.

15   (3) TRANSFER OF FUNDS TO DISBURSING

16 AGENT.—Funds received under subsection (a) by the

17 chief financial officer of any State shall be transferred

18 by such officer to the disbursing agent for such State

19 not less than 10 days after the date such officer re-

20 ceives such funds.

21   (4) PAYMENT BY DISBURSING AGENT.—A Na-

22 tional Dividend Payment shall be paid by the disburs-

23 ing agent of each State to each qualified registered

24 voter of such State who is included on a list provided

25 to such agent by the chief financial officer of such

State. Such payment shall be in the form of a negotiable instrument—

> (A) which is drawn on an account of such agent,
>
> (B) which is made payable to such voter, and
>
> (C) which states, on the endorsement side of such instrument, that—
>
>> (i) such instrument must be negotiated within the 90-day period which begins on the date such instrument is drawn,
>>
>> (ii) each qualified registered voter is entitled to only 1 National Dividend Payment for each calendar year, and
>>
>> (iii) any individual who negotiates any such instrument and who is not entitled to the payment made by such instrument is subject under Federal law to fine, or imprisonment, or both.

(5) NATIONAL DIVIDEND PAYMENT INSTALLMENTS.—

> (A) SEMIANNUAL INSTALLMENTS.—One-half of the amount of the National Dividend Payment payable during the 3 calendar years immediately following the Base Year to any qualified registered voter shall be paid to such voter at the

1   close of the second and fourth calendar quarters of

2   such year.

3   (B) QUARTERLY INSTALLMENTS.—One-

4   fourth of the National Dividend Payment payable

5   to any qualified registered voter during any calen-

6   dar year subsequent to the third calendar year fol-

7   lowing the Base Year shall be paid to such voter

8   at the close of each calendar quarter of such year.

9 (d) QUALIFIED REGISTERED VOTER.—

10   (1) IN GENERAL.—For purposes of this section,

11 an individual is a qualified registered voter for any cal-

12 endar year if—

13   (A) such individual was entitled to vote in

14   the most recent Federal election before such cal-

15   endar year, and

16   (B) such individual certifies to the State or

17   local authority which supervises the voting of

18   such individual that, during such calendar year,

19   he complies with all conditions of his entitlement

20   to vote.

21   (2) REGISTERED VOTERS.—In the case of any

22 individual who in any calendar year registers to vote

23 under State or local law, such registration shall be

24 treated as complying with the certification under para-

25 graph (1)(B) for such year.

1   (e) APPLICATIONS PERMITTED.—

2   (1) IN GENERAL.—The chief financial officer of

3   each State may require individuals to apply to receive

4   any National Dividend Payment under this Act.

5   (2) CRIMINAL PENALTY.—Any person who know-

6   ingly makes any false statement or false representation

7   of a material fact in any application submitted pursuant

8   to paragraph (1) or any certification under subsection

9   (d) shall be fined not more than $10,000, or imprisoned

10   not more than 10 years, or both for each such false

11   statement or false representation.

12   (f) PAYMENTS TO BE MADE FROM NATIONAL DIVI-

13 DEND PAYMENT TRUST FUND.—Amounts in the National

14 Dividend Payment Trust Fund shall be available, to such

15 extent and in such amounts as are provided in appropriation

16 Acts, for making the payments under this section.

17 SEC. 3. ESTABLISHMENT OF NATIONAL DIVIDEND PAYMENT

18   TRUST FUND.

19   (a) CREATION OF TRUST FUND.—There is hereby es-

20 tablished in the Treasury of the United States a trust fund to

21 be known as the National Dividend Payment Trust Fund.

22   (b) TRANSFER OF AMOUNTS EQUIVALENT TO CORPO-

23 RATE INCOME TAXES TO THE TRUST FUND.—

24   (1) IN GENERAL.—There are hereby authorized to

25   be appropriated to the Trust Fund amounts determined

1   by the Secretary to be equivalent to amounts received

2   in the Treasury in fiscal years ending after the Base

3   Year from the following taxes:

4   (A) the taxes imposed by sections 11, 511(a)

5   and 1201(a) of the Code;

6   (B) the taxes imposed by subchapter L of

7   chapter 1 of the Code; and

8   (C) the tax imposed on a corporation by sec-

9   tion 55(a) of the Code.

10   (2) TRANSITION RULE.—In the case of the first

11   four fiscal years ending after the Base Year, the

12   amounts authorized to be appropriated to the Trust

13   Fund for such years shall be the following percentage

14   of the amount determined under paragraph (1):

15   (A) 20 percent in the case of the first such

16   fiscal year;

17   (B) 40 percent in the case of the second such

18   fiscal year;

19   (C) 60 percent in the case of the third such

20   fiscal year; and

21   (D) 80 percent in the case of the fourth such

22   fiscal year.

23   (3) METHOD OF TRANSFER.—The amounts ap-

24   propriated pursuant to paragraphs (1) and (2) shall be

25   transferred at least quarterly from the general fund of

1 the Treasury to the Trust Fund on the basis of esti-

2 mates made by the Secretary of the amounts derived

3 from the taxes described in paragraph (1). Proper ad-

4 justments shall be made in the amounts subsequently

5 transferred to the extent such estimates are in excess

6 of or less than the amounts required to be transferred.

7   (4) TRANSFER FROM TRUST FUND FOR ADMINIS-

8 TRATIVE EXPENSES.—The Secretary may from time

9 to time transfer from the Trust Fund—

10   (A) to the general fund of the Treasury the

11   amount estimated as the costs incurred by the

12   Department of the Treasury in the administration

13   of section 2, and

14   (B) to the Board the amount estimated by

15   the Board as its costs in carrying out its duties

16   under this Act.

17 Proper adjustments shall be made in the amounts sub-

18 sequently transferred to the extent such estimates are

19 in excess of or less than the amounts required to be

20 transferred.

21 (c) TRUST FUND BOARD.—

22   (1) IN GENERAL.—There is hereby established a

23 review board to be known as the National Dividend

24 Review Board which shall consist of 5 members ap-

25 pointed by the President, by and with the advice and

1   consent of the Senate, from among individuals who are

2   not officers or employees of the Federal Government.

3   (2) DUTIES.—

4   (A) REPORT.—It shall be the duty of the

5   Board to review the manner in which payments

6   under section 2 are made, to hold the Trust Fund,

7   and to report to the Congress each year on such

8   review and on the financial condition and the re-

9   sults of the operations of the Trust Fund during

10   the preceding fiscal year and on its expected con-

11   dition and operation during the next 5 fiscal

12   years. Such report shall be printed as a House

13   document of the session of the Congress to which

14   the report is made.

15   (B) INVESTMENT.—

16   (i) IN GENERAL.—The Board may

17   invest any amount of the Trust Fund which

18   the Board determines is not required to meet

19   current payments. Such investments shall be

20   made only in interest-bearing obligations of

21   the United States or in obligations guaran-

22   teed as to both principal and interest by the

23   United States. Such obligations may be ac-

24   quired—

1   (I) on original issue at the issue

2   price, or

3   (II) by purchase of outstanding ob-

4   ligations at the market price.

5   The purposes for which obligations of the

6   United States may be issued under the

7   Second Liberty Bond Act are hereby ex-

8   tended to authorize the issuance at par of

9   special obligations exclusively to the Trust

10   Fund. Such special obligations shall bear in-

11   terest at a rate equal to the average rate of

12   interest, computed as to the end of the calen-

13   dar month next preceding the date of such

14   issue, borne by all marketable interest-bear-

15   ing obligations of the United States then

16   forming a part of the public debt; except that

17   if such average rate is not a multiple of one-

18   eighth of 1 percent, the rate of interest of

19   such special obligations shall be the multiple

20   of one-eighth of 1 percent next lower than

21   such average rate. Such special obligations

22   shall be issued only if the Board determines

23   that the purchase of other interest-bearing

24   obligations guaranteed as to both principal

25   and interest by the United States on original

1   issue or at the market price, is not in the

2   public interest.

3   (ii) SALE OF OBLIGATIONS.—Any obli-

4   gations acquired by the Trust Fund (except

5   special obligations issued exclusively to the

6   Trust Fund) may be sold by the Board at the

7   market price, and such special obligations

8   may be redeemed at par plus accrued in-

9   terest.

10   (iii) INTEREST ON CERTAIN PRO-

11   CEEDS.—The interest on, and the proceeds

12   from the sale or redemption of, any obliga-

13   tions held in the Trust Fund shall be credited

14   to and form a part of the Trust Fund.

15   (3) TERM, PAY, AND TRAVEL EXPENSES OF

16 MEMBERS.—

17   (A) TERM.—Each member of the Board

18   shall be appointed for a term of 2 years; except

19   that any member appointed to fill a vacancy oc-

20   curring before the expiration of the term for

21   which his predecessor was appointed shall be ap-

22   pointed only for the remainder of such term.

23   (B) PAY.—Members of the Board shall re-

24   ceive compensation at the rate of $100 for each

1   day they are engaged in the performance of their

2   duties as members of the Board.

3   (C) TRAVEL EXPENSES.—While away from

4   their homes or regular places of business in per-

5   formance of services for the Board, members of

6   the Board shall be allowed travel expenses, in-

7   cluding a per diem in lieu of subsistence, in the

8   same manner as persons employed intermittently

9   in the Government service are allowed expenses

10   under section 5703 of title 5 of the United States

11   Code.

12   (d) RESTRICTION ON THE USE OF THE TRUST

13 FUND.—Except as provided in subsection (b)(4), amounts in

14 the Trust Fund shall be available only for purposes of making

15 payments under section 2.

16 **SEC. 4. ELIMINATION OF DOUBLE TAX ON DIVIDENDS.**

17   (a) DIVIDENDS RECEIVED BY INDIVIDUALS.—

18   (1) IN GENERAL.—Part III of subchapter B of

19   chapter 1 of the Code (relating to items specifically ex-

20   cluded from gross income) is amended by inserting

21   after section 115 the following new section:

1 "SEC. 116. EXCLUSION OF DIVIDENDS RECEIVED BY INDIVID-

2   UALS.

3   "(a) EXCLUSION.—Gross income does not include

4 amounts received by an individual as dividends from domestic

5 corporations.

6   "(b) NATIONAL DIVIDEND PAYMENT.—For purposes of

7 subsection (a), amounts received by an individual as national

8 dividend payments under the National Dividend Act of 1987

9 shall be treated as dividends from domestic corporations."

10   (2) TECHNICAL, CONFORMING, AND CLERICAL

11   AMENDMENTS.—

12   (A) The table of sections for part III of sub-

13   chapter B of chapter 1 of the Code is amended by

14   inserting after the item relating to section 115 the

15   following new item:

"Sec. 116. Exclusion of dividends received by individuals."

16   (B) Subsection (g) of section 301 of the Code

17   (relating to special rules for distributions of prop-

18   erty by corporations) is amended by inserting after

19   paragraph (3) the following new paragraph (4):

20   "(4) For exclusion from gross income of dividends

21 received by individuals, see section 116."

22   (C) Subsection (a) of section 643 of the Code

23   (relating to certain definitions with respect to the

24   taxation of estates, trusts and beneficiaries) is

1   amended by inserting after paragraph (6) the fol-

2   lowing new paragraph (7):

3   "(7) DIVIDENDS.—There shall be included the

4 amount of any dividends excluded from gross income

5 pursuant to section 116 (relating to exclusion of divi-

6 dends)."

7 (b) DIVIDENDS RECEIVED BY CORPORATIONS.—

8   (1) IN GENERAL.—Subsection (a) of section 243

9   of the Code (relating to dividends received by corpora-

10   tions) is amended to read as follows:

11 "(a) GENERAL RULE.—In the case of a corporation,

12 there shall be allowed as a deduction an amount equal to 100

13 percent of the amount received as dividends from a domestic

14 corporation which is subject to taxation under this chapter."

15   (2) DIVIDENDS ON CERTAIN PREFERRED

16   STOCK.—Section 244 of the Code (relating to divi-

17   dends received on certain preferred stock) is amended

18   to read as follows:

19 "SEC. 244. DIVIDENDS RECEIVED ON CERTAIN PREFERRED

20   STOCK.

21 "In the case of a corporation, there shall be allowed as

22 a deduction an amount computed as follows:

23   "(1) First determine the amount received as divi-

24   dends on the preferred stock of a public utility which is

25   subject to taxation under this chapter and with respect

1 to which the deduction provided in section 247 for divi-

2 dends paid is allowable.

3 "(2) Then multiply the amount determined under

4 paragraph (1) by the fraction—

5 "(A) the numerator of which is 14 percent,

6 and

7 "(B) the denominator of which is that per-

8 centage which equals the highest rate of tax spec-

9 ified in section 11(b).

10 "(3) Finally ascertain the amount which is 100

11 percent of the excess of—

12 "(A) the amount determined under paragraph

13 (1), over

14 "(B) the amount determined under paragraph

15 (2)."

16 (3) TECHNICAL, CONFORMING AND CLERICAL

17 AMENDMENTS.—

18 (A) Section 243 of the Code (relating to divi-

19 dends received by corporations) is amended by

20 striking out subsection (b) and by redesignating

21 subsections (c) and (d) as subsections (b) and (c),

22 respectively.

23 (B) Subsection (b) of section 246 of the Code

24 (relating to rules applying to deductions for divi-

25 dends received) is amended by striking out

1   "243(a)(1), 244(a)" each time it appears and in-
2   serting in lieu thereof "243, 244" and by striking
3   out "80 percent of".

4   (C)(i) Subparagraph (A) of section 805(a)(4)
5   of the Code (relating to dividends received by life
6   insurance companies) is amended by striking out
7   all that follows "subparagraph (B))" and insert in
8   lieu thereof a period.

9   (ii) Subparagraph (B) of section 805(a)(4) of
10   the Code is amended—

11   (I) by striking out "243(A)(1), 244(a)"
12   each place it appears and inserting in lieu
13   thereof "243, 244", and

14   (II) by striking out "80 percent of".

15   (iii) Paragraph (4) of section 805(a) of the
16   Code is amended by striking out subparagraphs
17   (C) and (D) and inserting in lieu thereof the fol-
18   lowing:

19   "(C) DISTRIBUTIONS OUT OF TAX EXEMPT
20   INTEREST.—No deduction shall be allowed by
21   reason of this paragraph with respect to any divi-
22   dend to the extent the dividend is a distribution
23   out of tax-exempt interest."

24   (D) Subparagraph (C) of section 861(a)(2) of
25   the Code (relating to income from sources within

1   the United States) is amended by striking out

2   "243(d)" and inserting in lieu thereof "243(c)".

3   (E) Subparagraph (B) of section 1504(c)(2) of

4   the Code (relating to definition of includible insur-

5   ance companies) is amended by striking out clause

6   (i) and by redesignating clauses (ii) and (iii) as

7   clauses (i) and (ii), respectively.

8   (c) EFFECTIVE DATE.—The amendments made by this

9 section shall apply to taxable years ending after the date of

10 the enactment of this Act.

11 **SEC. 5. LIMITATION ON CORPORATE INCOME TAXES AND ON**

12   **NEW FEDERAL SPENDING.**

13   (a) LIMITATION ON CORPORATE INCOME TAXES.—

14 Notwithstanding any other provision of law, the maximum

15 rate of tax imposed by section 11 of the Code shall not be

16 increased above 34 percent.

17   (b) LIMITATION ON FEDERAL SPENDING.—Section

18 301 of the Congressional Budget and Impoundment Control

19 Act of 1974 is amended by inserting after subsection (i) the

20 following new subsection (j):

21   "(j) LIMITATION ON FEDERAL SPENDING.—

22   "(1) BUDGET RESOLUTIONS, ETC.—It shall not be

23   in order in either the House of Representatives or the

24   Senate to consider any concurrent resolution on the

25   budget for a fiscal year beginning after September 30,

1 1988 under this section or to consider any amendment
2 to such concurrent resolution or to consider a confer-
3 ence report on such concurrent resolution if the level of
4 total budget outlays for such fiscal year in such concur-
5 rent resolution or amendment or conference report ex-
6 ceeds the recommended level of total budget outlays in
7 the concurrent resolution under this section for the
8 fiscal year beginning October 1, 1987.

9   "(2) CONTINUING RESOLUTION.—For purposes of
10 paragraph (1), a joint resolution making appropriations
11 of money out of the Treasury not otherwise appropri-
12 ated and out of other applicable revenues, receipts and
13 funds shall be treated as a concurrent resolution on the
14 budget."

15 **SEC. 6. CALCULATION OF DEFICIT ADJUSTMENT AMOUNT.**

16   The amount to be deducted under section 2(b)(1)(B)(ii) of
17 this Act as the deficit adjustment in any calendar year shall
18 be the amount, if any, by which total budget outlays exceed
19 Federal revenues for the fiscal year ending in such calendar
20 year.

21 **SEC. 7. DEFINITIONS.**

22   For purposes of this Act—

23   (1) BASE YEAR.—The term "Base Year" means
24   the first calendar year after 1987 in which ends a

1   fiscal year in which total budget outlays do not exceed

2   Federal revenues.

3   (2) BOARD.—The term "Board" means the

4   National Dividend Review Board established by

5   section 3(c).

6   (3) FEDERAL ELECTION.—The term "Federal

7   election" means any general election in which Mem-

8   bers of (including any Delegate or Resident Commis-

9   sioner to) Congress are elected or in which the Presi-

10   dent and Vice President are elected.

11   (4) CODE.—The term "Code" means the Internal

12   Revenue Code of 1986.

13   (5) NATIONAL DIVIDEND PAYMENT.—The term

14   "National Dividend Payment" means the amount de-

15   termined under section 2(b).

16   (6) SECRETARY.—The term "Secretary" means

17   the Secretary of the Treasury or his delegate.

18   (7) STATE.—The term "State" includes the Dis-

19   trict of Columbia, the Commonwealth of Puerto Rico,

20   and any territory or possession of the United States.

21   (8) TRUST FUND.—The term "Trust Fund"

22   means the National Dividend Payment Trust Fund es-

23   tablished by section 3(a).

○

THE NATIONAL DIVIDEND PLAN

In July of 1983, Congressman Thomas J. Downey (D) New York, Chairman of the Task Force on Tax Policy of the House Budget Committee, U.S. House of Representatives, wrote to John H. Perry, Jr., seeking his views on the key issues of tax policy and the federal deficit. Mr. Perry agreed to present his ideas. His testimony was listened to and, more than that, it was acted on. It is best to start with that testimony in developing an understanding of the issues, the Plan and the Bill......

Statement of

JOHN H. PERRY, JR.

Chairman, Perry Oceanographics, Inc.

Perry Cable TV, Inc.

to the

TASK FORCE ON TAX POLICY

OF THE

HOUSE BUDGET COMMITTEE

U. S. HOUSE OF REPRESENTATIVES

August 1, 1983

My name is John H. Perry, Jr. and I am here in response to Chairman Downey's letter to me of July 25. I am happy to reply to his three questions, and I quote:

1.—"We would be particularly interested in hearing your reaction to the growing dissatisfaction of the present tax system as evidenced by unprecedented non-compliance.

2.—"Your views for overhauling our current approach and, in particular

3.—"How your suggestions might aid the Congress in lowering the budget deficit."

67

Now To Reply:

1. In regard to growing evidence of non-compliance, it is my considered opinion, having been a faithful tax-payer for over 40 years, that the overwhelming majority of our citizens seriously want to do their fair share towards the upkeep of their government but that some of them balk on occasion due to one of several factors. They don't mind paying the tax so long as the money is used prudently, that it is not being used to keep them from earning money. When they hear or see evidence of graft and waste or inefficiency in government they feel cheated and non-compliance is a way of cheating back or getting even. Taxing beyond the point of diminishing returns for punitive purposes is one of the significant reasons. If they felt the tax money they are paying would more directly, more efficiently benefit the less well off, they would have less antipathy to transfer payments. But to label these payments as entitlements really raises their anger. Non-compliance is their own "entitlement program." This leads us to Question No. 2: Overhauling the tax structure.

The first point to consider is to make sure that the tax laws and their rates produce the most revenue. If the tax rate is too high it will not only produce less revenue than otherwise, it will encourage the tax payer to go underground or to spend most of his time trying to utilize tax shelters or other tax avoidance schemes. Recent tax history has proven this. Therefore, what we are looking for is a mechanism which will provide our society with the greatest good for the greatest number; to encourage the producers to work for society as a whole and for those unable to produce either due to intellect, age, health or whatever reason. But we must above all have a mechanism that will be simple, honest, fair and directly responsive to the voter. Before going into details I would like to point out that in order to achieve these social goals we must first have a stable, profitable economy.

Our major problem today is an uncertain economy. It is uncertain because the federal budget appears to be out of control. For more than three years there has been virtually no real growth in economic activity in the United States. As long as that condition exists, it can only mean continued high unemployment, continued inflation, high interest rates and no real profits.

Without real profits there can be no prosperity, no full employment, no advances in technology, no improvement in our competitive world trade position and no real, earned money to support the government. Without a restructuring of the federal government's financial obligations, we cannot restore confidence in Wall Street or in the consumer, and, therefore, we cannot have recovery that we can count on.

How did we get into this critical situation? Plainly stated, by using a philosophy of stimulating the economy through demand-side economics, we took on more federal programs than we could afford. Let me make it clear that I intend no criticism of the motives or goals of those who promoted and implemented these programs. Their motives and goals were sincere and well-intentioned. However, the fact is that even the best programs may have features built into them that create destructive side effects over a long period. One of those side effects was rampant inflation, and we turned from demand-side to supply-side economics to reduce and bring it under control. But when we reduced inflation, we also reduced personal income tax bracket creep, and that choked off federal revenues, aggravating already serious budget deficits. In addition, increases in military spending, and indexing of welfare and Social Security threw the budget even further out of control. And this has paved the way for more debt and deficits which will send inflation soaring again because there is an undeniable connection between the amount of our federal debt and the Consumer Price Index (CPI). And while the recent recession lowered the CPI somewhat, it is already back up to where it was before the decline.

• We need a politically feasible way to curb the forces which cause the federal budget to remain in deficit.

• We must separate management of the debt from management of the humanely-motivated social programs of the last half century before they fall victim to a massive financial crunch.

• We must have both supply-side and demand-side economics.

I believe the National Dividend Plan is a major step in the direction of a sound national economic footing. I also believe that the members of this Task Force will concur when they learn of its provisions and potentialities.

The National Dividend Plan provides a new way of conducting United States fiscal policy. It creates incentives for politicians to respond to the public and to conduct the budgetary policy of the nation on a sounder basis. It also creates incentives for cooperation between business and the consumer, because under this legislation the more profitable business becomes, the greater the benefits received by the public. The public's primary benefits are job security and enhancement of society's real wealth.

There are other direct, individual benefits, too. However, before getting into them, we should examine the basic framework of the plan.

There are five basic tenets of the National Dividend Plan:

1. A National Dividend Trust Fund would be set up. All federal corporate income tax collections would be placed in this trust fund. These funds would be held in trust for all legally registered United States voters and would be distributed as dividends on a quarterly, per capita basis to those voters. These dividends would be exempt from federal taxes.

2. To ensure that there would be no further federal budget deficits, the registered voter would, in effect, be paying for any

deficit because he or she would not get the full national pro rata dividend unless the government first earned a surplus. In Treasury jargon this is called "statutory ratcheting."

3. Double taxation on corporate dividends would be eliminated. Dividends paid by corporations to stockholders would not be taxed as personal income. Thus, dividends received through the National Dividend Act and through stock ownership would be exempt from any federal tax. This provides strong incentive for job-creating investment in the private sector. It also eliminates or greatly simplifies more than 50 sections of the tax code.

4. Maximum corporate tax rates would be frozen at the current 46 percent level. This is designed to enable members of the Congress to resist any possible political pressure to increase the corporate tax rate for larger dividends which, in turn, would result in going beyond the point of diminishing return. Such tax rate increases would destroy all incentives to business and would drain the vitality from the producers.

5. A five-year moratorium would be imposed on federal budget increases. The Plan would prohibit the Congress for the first five years of the dividend from considering any budget resolution that would increase total budget outlays beyond the level of the fiscal year in which the bill is enacted. During this initial five-year period, corporate tax revenues would be paid into the trust fund in increments of 20 percent per year, since the problem of paying for current deficits still exists. The five-year moratorium on federal budget increases and the five-year incremental funding of the trust fund are designed to allow revenues to catch up with expenditures as the economy grows over that period.

Administration of the Trust Fund would be done through the banking system. Payment to local banks for servicing the trust fund would be implicit. By allowing the banks to maintain the deposits until payment, this would give them interest free money for a limited amount of time. That should give them incentive for taking on the deposits and administering the fund.

The National Dividend Plan's use of the nation's registered voters on a per capita basis as a distribution system for the dividend payments is based upon this reasoning:

First, voting records already are maintained in every community throughout the country. This eliminates any need for setting up a huge, costly agency to do the job. Second, the voting system assures equality of treatment for all without regard to sex, race, creed or national origin. It removes political pressures and bureaucratic manipulation as factors in the distribution process. Third, by checking voter registration signatures in poll books with voter endorsements of national dividend checks, election officials will be able to eliminate fraudulent voting practices where suspicions are strong enough to commit the resources needed to cross check. And, fourth, since each registered voter will receive the same amount, there will be no necessity to involve the costly overhead of the federal government in the distribution of the dividend.

The National Dividend Plan provides an alternative to current fiscal operations that contains a different set of incentives than the present system. The current fiscal operation, although developed along desirable social guidelines, has presented an incentive system to the public and to the government itself, that has been detrimental to the economy over the long term. The National Dividend Plan seeks to correct this incentive system while implementing a program where private enterprise is encouraged and the needy are not forgotten.

The National Dividend Plan's provisions do not depend upon the particular form of the tax system. The present progressive tax system with a multitude of exemptions is compatible, as is the new idea of a proportional income tax system with very few exemptions. The precise income tax system is not the crucial thing. If a proportional income tax system were introduced without the National

Dividend Plan, it would still contain all the incentive problems of the current system and the present environment would still exist.

A proportional tax is aimed at simplifying the reporting system and reducing the tax load on larger incomes so the incentive to use tax shelters or not report income is lessened. The National Dividend Plan is designed to make all of the people feel that they benefit from the economic system, from business and not necessarily from government. It has to do with corporate taxes, not personal income taxes.

The source of the money and the success of the program embraced in the National Dividend Plan are dependent on the same force, the productive abilities of American business. As business grows and profits, the consumer benefits because he or she will receive larger dividend payments.

The public will begin to conduct its affairs on a more prudent basis as it perceives that the government is conducting its affairs more soundly. A significant change in the operation of the government can result in a significant change in the behavior of the public as well. Less prudent fiscal behavior on the part of the government has led to less prudent fiscal behavior on the part of the American public.

There are other potential benefits in the program offered by the National Dividend Plan. **Reduced inflation rates should result in lower inflationary expectations**. And that, in turn, should bring lower interest rates and more efforts to expand production activities because the potential for economic gain in speculation will drop relative to that which can be earned from production.

Labor-business problems should be eased because with a lessening of inflationary pressures, the antagonistic relationship between labor and business should be reduced. In addition, labor benefits from the National Dividend Plan's program, so it is in the interest of labor for business to be successful.

There are two points of major importance about the National Dividend Plan's provisions which should be emphasized. They are:

1. No funds would be distributed to the registered voters that had not been earned; as long as we have profitable productivity and a federal government operating without deficits, we will have national dividend payments.

2. The National Dividend Plan in no way disturbs the property rights of corporation owners, the shareholders. It simply calls for a different, more direct, more efficient way of distributing tax funds that already are being collected—and have been collected for years.

The National Dividend Plan offers the American voters a quid pro quo: A share in the nation's profits in exchange for a cap on federal expenses for the next five years. Having the voters as part of the capitalistic system will do more to reduce unemployment than any other factor. By encouraging both demand and supply economics for the benefit of the general welfare, we no longer will have to cut back on government spending or use other methods to reduce inflation at the expense of increased unemployment.

Necessary constituency support will be generated through the National Dividend Plan because American voters can get more benefits in the long run from their dividends, from a stable economy and from the knowledge that they are getting their fair share of what is available from corporate profits. It must become obvious to them that no one is entitled to any funds that have not been earned.

In some ways, our well-meaning policies of the past have attempted the philosophy of, "To each according to his need...," a policy which has committed us to more humanitarian programs than we can afford and thus jeopardized our free economic system. But, as a free society, we have always found the strength and wisdom to work our way out of the dilemmas and achieve even greater heights.

I believe that in our democratically based, capitalist society, our doctrine must be, "To each according to our free society's ability to pay and to encourage the producers to work for the benefit of us all."

A National Dividend Plan can achieve that necessary goal in a politically feasible manner because the electorate, the most powerful force in our society, will back it up.

Thank you.

TESTIMONY OF JOHN H. PERRY, JR. TO THE SENATE COMMITTEE ON FINANCE

September 20, 1984

In view of the current dilemma of whether or not to raise taxes, I thought it might be appropriate to call your attention to some recent press comments on H. R. 5085—the National Dividend Act. The attached AP column by John Cunniff does an excellent and succinct job of explaining the Act's advantages and also there is attached some editorial opinion on the subject.

As you know, there are now 35 sponsors on the bill, representing a very broad spectrum of House support to get the budget under control. Fourteen of the sponsors are on the Ways and Means Committee.

I suspect that the Administration is considering seeking a fundamental change in our tax system after the election. But in view of the complexity of our present tax system built up over decades with its carry-forwards and carry-backs and the rights of our citizens to challenge the constitutionality of any of the provisions, including such issues as fairness and protection of property rights, I do not believe that it is possible to make a fundamental change in the way our taxes are collected. It is much easier to change the way we spend the money than it is to change the way we collect the money.

Some ideas may sound good but the minute that you examine them, they fall apart—not necessarily because they are not good ideas, but because politically it is not feasible to make a drastic change.

On the other hand, H. R. 5085 does not attempt to tamper with the basic system. It merely changes the way the system pays out some of the tax collections and in a manner that is simple and one that increases incentives. In addition, it provides an answer to the fairness issue. The only change it makes in the collection part of the system is one which merely eliminates more than fifty tax code provisions.

Finally, most all of the new proposals fail to address themselves to the basic flaw that is causing all the fuss in the first place, i.e., excessive government spending and its role in the economy. None of them prevent the excesses and abuses which have caused the problem. They address themselves to the problem of raising more money faster so as to cure the twin demons of debt and deficit. If one or the other of the proposed systems were in effect, the old "tax, tax, spend, spend, elect, elect" syndrome would still be at work but more guilty than ever because it would then be so easy to solve the shortages by merely raising the percentages.

We dare not forget a fundamental requirement—we need earnings in real dollars to pay for the transfer payments, the entitlements, the "bread and circuses" or else we are going down the same old route that has been responsible for the collapse of so many preceding civilizations—never in the history of the entire world has a solution to this problem been more important and urgently needed.

The time is ripe to have this concept given serious consideration. The voters will be overwhelmingly behind you since money that formerly was used to build up the bureaucrats' power will now be going directly to them. This plan will not require a constitutional amendment but will accomplish the same end result with added political dividends.

EVERY DAY that the Congress delays in passing H. R. 5085, it costs the federal government ONE-HALF BILLION DOLLARS, because that is the current daily cost of our annual deficits. The National Dividend Act would stop the deficits because the voters would insist on it, so that they could receive their national dividends.

TESTIMONY OF

BILLY LEE EVANS

For

AMERICANS FOR THE NATIONAL DIVIDEND ACT

To

THE TAX REFORM STUDY HEARINGS

OF THE

U. S. DEPARTMENT OF THE TREASURY

June 26, 1984

My name is Billy Lee Evans and I am a partner in the firm of Alcalde, Henderson and O'Bannon in Arlington, Virginia. Before joining my present firm, I spent six years in the United States Congress from the State of Georgia after having served in the Georgia State Legislature for eight years. My experience in both public and private life has taught me that not all good ideas come from government. For that reason I applaud this administration for that recognition and for taking the initiative to seek out ideas from the public that may enable the government to institute a tax policy that is both simple and fair.

What I offer today is certainly an idea whose time has come. I refer to the National Dividend Plan. This Plan has withstood the careful analysis and scrutiny of professionals in academics, finance, economics, banking, the social sciences and politics, to name but a few. The author of this Plan, John H. Perry, Jr., has spent many years and millions of dollars in a careful and detailed analysis of his proposal before it was offered in legislative form. It has been introduced in the current session of Congress as H. R. 5085 and its thirty-five (35) co-sponsors are as representative of the political and social diversity of this nation as possible.

While the National Dividend Plan would not address personal income taxes, it will create the most favorable possible economic conditions for a fair and equitable application of taxes.

Mr. Chairman, I would like to summarize the elements of the National Dividend Plan at this time. I have provided for the record more detailed information including a copy of the bill, H. R. 5085.

CREATING A CONSTITUENCY FOR REAL ECONOMIC GROWTH

The National Dividend Plan is a comprehensive economic proposal to revitalize the most powerful economic machine in history—the American Economy—and to allow all of our citizens to participate and benefit from this success. The Plan accomplishes this by instituting five related reforms that will encourage participation in the private sector and assure a balanced federal budget.

These five reforms are the heart of the National Dividend Act, H. R. 5085, now pending before Congress.

1. *NATIONAL PROFIT SHARING*—The central innovation of the Plan is the creation of the National Dividend Trust Fund. All federal corporate income tax collections would be placed in this Trust. Instead of being spent as part of the government budget, the fund would be distributed in quarterly dividends to all registered voters—so long as the federal deficit did not exceed the amount in the Trust. Dividend payments would increase as corporate productivity increased.

   Funds would be distributed through local banks using local voter registration lists. Banks would be compensated for the expenses involved by serving as interest free depositories for specified short periods of time.

While the dividend payments would be exempt from federal taxes, they could be subject to state and local taxes (at the discretion of state and local governments). This additional revenue could enable states and cities to operate with no new taxes.

2. *DISCOURAGING BUDGET DEFICITS*—Total funds available for the National Dividend would be reduced each year by any federal budget deficit. This feature is called the Automatic Dividend Deduction (ADD). The ADD provision of the National Dividend Plan gives every voter a vested, self-interest reason for resisting federal deficits. A federal deficit would become a major political liability to a member of Congress, because that member would be held directly responsible for the reduction or absence of his constituents' dividend checks.

3. *ELIMINATE DOUBLE TAXATION OF DIVIDENDS*—Corporate profits presently are taxed twice by the federal government, first at the corporate level and again on the individual level when distributed to shareholders as dividends. Such a tax creates a disincentive to invest.

The National Dividend Plan would end federal personal income tax on corporate dividends. This would attract investment dollars into the private sector, thus creating new jobs and stimulating economic growth.

4. *A CAP ON CORPORATE TAX RATES*—The National Dividend Plan addresses the issue of placing a ceiling on the federal corporate income tax rate. The plan is flexible on the level which

the cap would establish. However, it suggests that the rate should not exceed 46 percent, the current rate.

Placing a statutory ceiling on tax rates is a necessary check against the "self-interest" of voters whose dividends, in the short run, would increase in direct relation to an increase in the corporate tax rate.

5. *CONTROL GOVERNMENT EXPANSION*—The National Dividend Plan would be phased in over a five-year period. To prevent disruption of existing federal programs during this time, a moratorium would be placed on new federal spending programs. The moratorium would permit revenues, increasing from normal economic growth, to catch up with current spending levels without threatening existing government services.

In the first year, one-fifth of all corporate income taxes would be paid into the Trust Fund. In the second year, two-fifths, and so on. In the fifth year the program would be fully operational.

The Plan requires no new taxes and would be funded entirely by earned dollars, as opposed to tax or deficit dollars. No additional layer of bureaucracy would be required to administer the Plan, since all money would be distributed through private banks.

Most important of all, the National Dividend Plan would guarantee a majority constituency against excessive government spending and would reward productivity of the American people.

The NDP is a recognition of the fact that this country's economic problems are not caused by flaws in the science of economics. They are the unquestionable result of our political system which weighs the political impact among varied interest groups of this nation to laws pertaining to our methods of financing government.

82

We believe the National Dividend Plan is unique in that it will treat the entire electorate in the same unbiased way. It will provide the incentive for the electorate to permit Congress to take the necessary (and unprecedented) steps to cap spending until revenues catch up.

STATE BY STATE ESTIMATES OF NATIONAL DIVIDEND PLAN'S ECONOMIC IMPACT WHEN FULLY IMPLEMENTED

STATE	1986 Registered Voters	Voting Age Population	% of VAP Registered
AL	2362361	2949000	80.11%
AK	292274	373000	78.36%
AZ	1597934	2399000	66.61%
AR	1188831	1729000	68.76%
CA	12883920	19811000	65.03%
CO	1817370	2432000	74.73%
CT	1670798	2445000	68.34%
DE	296436	469000	63.21%
DC	280175	483000	58.01%
FL	5631188	9111000	61.81%
GA	2575815	4402000	58.51%
HI	419794	782000	53.68%
ID	549934	705000	78.00%
IL	6004515	8490000	70.72%
IN	2878498	4033000	71.37%
IA	1621538	2115000	76.67%
KS	1172670	1809000	64.82%
KY	1998889	2728000	73.27%
LA	2179317	3186000	68.40%
ME	790083	874000	90.40%
MD	2139690	3333000	64.20%
MA	3005729	4525000	66.42%
MI	5790753	6633000	87.30%
MN	2615137	3098000	84.41%
MS	1643192	1833000	89.64%

Total NDP Payout with plan in full operation	Economic Impact (Multiplyer of 3.3)	Increased Personal Savings from Payout	STATE
$1,949,715,283.14	$6,176,698,016.99	$116,982,916.99	AL
$241,221,000.80	$764,188,130.53	$14,473,260.05	AK
$1,318,814,669.41	$4,178,004,872.70	$79,128,880.16	AZ
$981,171,789.48	$3,108,352,229.08	$58,870,307.37	AR
$10,633,419,587.76	$33,686,673,254.02	$638,005,175.27	CA
$1,499,920,657.39	$4,751,748,642.62	$89,995,239.44	CO
$1,378,951,140.68	$4,368,517,213.66	$82,737,068.44	CT
$244,656,002.90	$775,070,217.20	$14,679,360.17	DE
$231,235,395.21	$732,553,732.01	$13,874,123.71	DC
$4,647,559,499.09	$14,723,468,493.13	$278,853,569.95	FL
$2,125,884,177.75	$6,734,801,075.12	$127,553,050.67	GA
$346,466,428.11	$1,097,605,644.24	$20,787,985.69	HI
$453,874,206.57	$1,437,873,486.43	$27,232,452.39	ID
$4,955,675,556.51	$15,699,580,163.02	$297,340,533.39	IL
$2,375,695,985.11	$7,526,204,880.84	$142,541,759.11	IN
$1,338,295,637.62	$4,239,720,579.99	$80,297,738.26	IA
$967,833,714.27	$3,066,097,206.81	$58,070,022.86	KS
$1,649,732,802.31	$5,226,353,517.72	$98,983,968.14	KY
$1,798,644,517.80	$5,698,105,832.38	$107,918,671.07	LA
$652,075,148.57	$2,065,774,070.67	$39,124,508.91	ME
$1,765,939,369.21	$5,594,495,921.65	$105,956,362.15	MD
$2,480,702,893.54	$7,858,866,766.73	$148,842,173.61	MA
$4,779,252,461.83	$15,140,671,799.09	$286,755,147.71	MI
$2,158,337,602.26	$6,837,613,523.95	$129,500,256.14	MN
$1,356,167,222.34	$4,296,337,760.37	$81,370,033.34	MS

MO	2769184	3744000	73.96%
MT	443935	595000	74.61%
NE	849762	1177000	72.20%
NV	367579	724000	50.77%
NH	551257	765000	72.06%
NJ	3777278	5815000	64.96%
NM	632787	1035000	61.14%
NY	8072004	13472000	59.92%
NC	3080990	4748000	64.89%
ND	336600	495000	68.00%
OH	5924746	7891000	75.08%
OK	2018401	2445000	82.55%
OR	1502244	2016000	74.52%
PA	5846975	9023000	64.80%
RI	524664	750000	69.96%
SC	1298857	2467000	52.65%
SD	428097	509000	84.11%
TN	2543597	3563000	71.39%
TX	7287173	11891000	61.28%
UT	763057	1058000	72.12%
VT	327788	401000	81.74%
VA	2609698	4377000	59.62%
WA	2230354	3317000	67.24%
WV	946039	1435000	65.93%
WI	2390200	3515000	68.00%
WY	235292	360000	65.36%

TOTAL	121164409	174325000	69.50%

NOTE: Wisconsin and North Dakota do not have registration

$2,285,476,422.37	$7,240,389,306.07	$137,128,585.34	MO
$366,390,595.77	$1,160,725,407.41	$21,983,435.75	MT
$701,329,711.43	$2,221,812,525.82	$42,079,782.69	NE
$303,372,090.07	$961,082,781.33	$18,202,325.40	NV
$454,966,111.38	$1,441,332,640.84	$27,297,966.68	NH
$3,117,481,470.98	$9,876,181,300.07	$187,048,888.26	NJ
$522,254,847.96	$1,654,503,358.33	$31,335,290.88	NM
$6,662,025,644.84	$21,105,297,242.86	$399,721,538.69	NY
$2,542,817,668.51	$8,055,646,373.85	$152,569,060.11	NC
$277,804,350.95	$880,084,183.80	$16,668,261.06	ND
$4,889,840,217.02	$15,491,013,807.53	$293,390,413.02	OH
$1,665,836,541.16	$5,277,370,162.39	$99,950,192.47	OK
$1,239,839,332.69	$3,927,811,005.95	$74,390,359.96	OR
$4,825,653,876.63	$15,287,671,481.15	$289,539,232.60	PA
$433,018,247.13	$1,371,801,806.92	$25,981,094.83	RI
$1,071,978,983.53	$3,396,029,419.83	$64,318,739.01	SC
$353,319,100.50	$1,119,314,910.37	$21,199,146.03	SD
$2,099,293,861.12	$6,650,562,952.03	$125,957,631.67	TN
$6,014,285,102.48	$19,053,255,204.67	$360,857,106.15	TX
$629,769,918.66	$1,995,111,102.30	$37,786,195.12	UT
$270,531,588.20	$857,044,071.42	$16,231,895.29	VT
$2,153,848,660.29	$6,823,392,555.81	$129,230,919.62	VA
$1,840,766,623.14	$5,831,548,662.12	$110,445,997.39	WA
$780,789,513.86	$2,473,541,179.90	$46,847,370.83	WV
$1,972,691,502.17	$6,249,486,678.88	$118,361,490.13	WI
$194,192,339.11	$615,201,330.29	$11,651,540.35	WY

$100,000,000,000.00 $316,800,000,000.00 $6,000,000,000.00   TOTAL

and are estimated at 68 percent.

87

SUMMARY OF
MARKET OPINION RESEARCH/
PETER HART POLL

The National Dividend Act: Survey Results

Few Americans have yet heard of H.R. 56 -- the National Dividend Act. But a recent national survey shows the legislation is supported by a majority of those who learn about the Act and its provisions.

The National Dividend Act (H.R. 56) proposes to distribute a portion of federal corporate income tax receipts in the form of periodic profit-sharing checks to all registered voters. Payouts would begin only after the federal budget reaches a surplus condition, and the authors of the Act say this would make a balanced budget politically more attractive.

The following tables summarize a March, 1986 telephone survey in which fifteen hundred Americans were presented the concept of the National Dividend Act and asked their opinions of it. The research was designed and the questionnaire developed jointly by Peter Hart Research Associates and Market Opinion Research. Sampling and field work were completed by Market Opinion Research at its facilities in Detroit, Michigan. A random sample of 1500 has a sampling error of approximately 3% at the 95% level of confidence.

The survey was commissioned by John H. Perry, Jr., a Florida industrialist who originally conceived of the National Dividend Act. Inquiries about the National Dividend Act should be made to David Henderson (703/841-0626). Questions about the research findings can be answered by Will Feltus at Market Opinion Research (202/293-7570) or by Peter Hart (202/234-5570).

THE ULTIMATE SELF INTEREST

SUMMARY TABLES

TABLE 1

Throughout the interview the legislation was called the "National Profit Sharing and Dividend Act" in order to make it easier for survey respondents to comprehend. Table 1 shows how the proposal was explained to the survey respondents. The Act was broken into its major components and respondents were asked whether each provision was or was not clear to them. As Table 1 indicates, relatively few respondents were unable to grasp the basic elements of the proposal.

TABLE 2

Respondents were twice asked their overall opinion of the national dividend proposal. The first such question came immediately after the initial explaination of the Act; the second question was asked late in the interview after respondents had been given an opportunity to become more familiar with the specific aspects of the proposal.

The results of the first question are shown in Table 2. By 56% to 31% margin, the majority of those surveyed approved of the National Profit Sharing and Dividend Act. Approval for the proposal is somewhat higher among Democrats than among Republicans. However, as will be shown later, attitudes about the National Dividend Act are much less partisan than opinions about Gramm-Rudman-Hollings.

MARKET OPINION RESEARCH/PETER HART POLL

<u>TABLES 3-4</u>

These questions explore in more depth respondents' opinions of the national profit sharing and dividend proposal. As indicated in Table 3, respondents felt strongly that a national dividend should be paid only after eliminating the deficit. Respondents also supported, but by smaller margins, paying a profit sharing dividend to all registered voters, regardless of their income level.

As shown in Table 4, a two-to-one majority agree with the premise that a national profit sharing dividend would encourage Congress to keep the federal budget balanced.

<u>TABLE 5</u>

After considering the proposal in more detail, a 64% to 23% majority felt that the national profit sharing and dividend act is a good idea which should be considered by Congress. The 39 point favorable margin on this question compares to a 25 point favorable margin when respondents were first asked their opinion of the Act. Table 5 also shows that voters would have a more favorable opinion of a congressional candidate who supports the National Dividend Act. Republican and Independent voters have a more impression of such a candidate by a two-to-one margin, while Democrats are more favorably inclined by a three-to-one ratio.

91

THE ULTIMATE SELF INTEREST

TABLES 6-9

These tables summarize respondents' volunteered opinions of the National Profit Sharing and Dividend Act. The combined responses in Table 7 -- which collapses similar responses from Table 6 -- show that those who feel the Act is a good idea see it as a way to balance the budget and hold down federal spending. In fact, respondents are twice as likely to cite balanced budget or spending mentions as they are to say that they would like to get their own dividend check.

Those who feel the proposal is a bad idea most often say that the bill is simply not workable and unlikely to pass Congress. They also feel it would not hold down federal spending and that paying out a national dividend would be another welfare program or government handout.

TABLES 10-11

Americans are skeptical that Congress would be able to keep the federal budget balanced. In an earlier question asked before the national dividend act was explained, a full 57% said that should Congress be able to balance the budget it would not be able to keep it balanced. However, after hearing about the National Dividend Act, a 54% to 36% majority feel that a proposal would help Congress keep the federal budget balanced.

Finally, Table 11 shows that 52% of those familiar with Gramm-Rudman-Hollings support it. However, opinions of Gramm-Rudman vary strongly across party lines -- 66% of the Republicans support Gramm-Rudman compared to only 35% of Democrats. The graph shows that opinions of the National Dividend Act are less strongly partisan.

MARKET OPINION RESEARCH/PETER HART POLL

TABLE 1

Now I'd like to explain a proposal called "The National Profit Sharing and Dividend Act." This act is designed to make it easier for Congress to keep the federal budget balanced. There are four main things this act would do. In order to make sure you understand this proposal, let me summarize each of its main points and I'd like you to tell me if each one is or is not clear to you?

	Clear	Not Clear	Don't Know	Refused/ NA
* (Under this act), all federal income taxes paid on corporation profits would be put in a separate trust fund at the U.S. Treasury each year.	77%	22%	1%	*%
* (Under this act), if there is a federal deficit in a given year, this trust fund would be used to pay the difference between what the government takes in and what it spends.	87	11	1	*
* (Under the act), any money which was left in the trust fund after paying the budget deficit would be paid out to all adult Americans as a national profit sharing dividend. All American citizens 18 years of age or older would receive a yearly profit sharing dividend check for as much as $900 per person. In years when the federal budget isn't balanced, there would be no money left in the corporate income tax trust fund and there would be no national profit sharing dividend paid that year.	86	13	1	*
* Because Americans would want to receive their national profit sharing dividend check, this act would make members of Congress much more reluctant to spend more than the government takes in.	87	12	1	*

93

THE ULTIMATE SELF INTEREST

TABLE 2

Based on what you understand about the National Profit Sharing
and Dividend Act, do you favor or oppose the proposal?

	Total	Rep.	Indep.	Dem.
Strongly favor	22%	21%	20%	24%
Just somewhat favor	34	31	35	37
Just somewhat oppose	14	15	16	13
Strongly oppose	17	20	15	14
Don't Know	12	13	14	11
Refused/NA	1	1	1	1
Total	100%	100%	100%	100%

Collapsed:

	Total	Rep.	Indep.	Dem.
Favor	56%	52%	54%	61%
Oppose	31	35	31	28
Total	100%	100%	100%	100%
*PDI	+25	+17	+23	+33

(*PDI=Percentage favor minus percentage oppose.)

MARKET OPINION RESEARCH/PETER HART POLL

TABLE 3

Now, I'd like to go over some of the specific provisions of the National Profit Sharing and Dividend Act, and have you tell me if you think each one is a good idea or a bad idea?

	Good Idea	Bad Idea	Don't Know	PDI[a]
In any year there is a federal deficit, money from the corporate trust fund would be used to pay off as much of the deficit as possible.	76%	20%	4%	+56
Federal income taxes paid on corporation profits would be put in a trust fund at the U.S. Treasury, and kept separate from income taxes paid by individuals.	62	27	11	+35
Money left in the trust fund after paying the deficit would be paid out as a national profit sharing dividend.	62	32	5	+30
The national profit sharing dividend would average as much as $900 per person each year.	61	33	6	+28
The profit sharing dividend would be paid to all adult American citizens, 18 years or older, who are registered to vote.	56	40	3	+16
The same national profit sharing dividend would be paid to all adult Americans, regardless of their income level.	53	43	4	+10

[a]PDI: Percentage Difference Index=% "Good idea" minus % "Bad idea."

THE ULTIMATE SELF INTEREST

TABLE 4

Here are some statements others have made about the National Profit Sharing and
Dividend Act, and, for each one, please tell me if you agree or disagree with
it.

	Agree	Neither Agree Nor Disagree and Don't Know	Disagree	PDI[a]
Corporations and business leaders are very likely to oppose the National Profit Sharing and Dividend Act.	78%	8%	13%	+65
Because Americans would want to receive a national profit sharing dividend check, members of Congress would become much more reluctant to spend more than the government takes in.	63	9	29	+34
If Congress is ever able to balance the federal budget, a national profit sharing dividend would help keep the federal budget balanced.	61	12	28	+33
Since Americans contribute to the profitability of corporations through their consumer purchases, it makes good sense to let Americans share in those corporate profits.	62	8	31	+31
Instead of paying a national profit sharing dividend, it would be better to let the U.S. government spend the corporate income tax revenues on federal projects and programs.	45	11	44	+1
The National Profit Sharing and Dividend Act is just another government giveaway program.	36	12	52	-16

96

MARKET OPINION RESEARCH/PETER HART POLL

TABLE 5

Based on what you've heard so far about the National Profit Sharing and Dividend Act, would you say that this proposal is a good idea which should be considered by Congress or a bad idea which should not be considered by Congress?

	Total	Rep.	Indep.	Dem.
Very good idea	26%	23%	25%	31%
Fairly good idea	38	36	36	40
Fairly bad idea	9	12	6	8
Very bad idea	14	17	14	12
Don't know	12	13	20	8
Refused/NA	*	*	1	1

Suppose a candidate for Congress supported the National Profit Sharing and Dividend Act -- would this give you a more favorable or less favorable impression of the candidate?

	Total	Rep.	Indep.	Dem.
More favorable	52%	49%	40%	59%
No difference	20	19	30	18
Less favorable	19	23	19	16
Don't know	8	8	10	7
Refused/NA	1	1	--	*

THE ULTIMATE SELF INTEREST

TABLE 6

Why do you think that the National Profit Sharing
and Dividend Act is a good idea?

Would balance the budget/Budget would be balanced/Help balance the budget	22%
People like to get money back from the government/Like to get a rebate/People would like getting a check	18
Gives them a chance to get involved/All of the people would benefit/Better for the people	9
Cut spending/Cut federal spending/Cut government spending	8
Sounds good/Sounds fair/It is fair/Good/Would be fair	8
Corporations are not paying their fair share/Make corporations pay fair share	6
Would cut wasteful spending on programs not needed/Would make Congress stop spending on unnecessary programs	4
Makes government responsible for spending/Holds government accountable	4
Other	21
Total	100%

MARKET OPINION RESEARCH/PETER HART POLL

TABLE 7

Why do you think that the National Profit Sharing
and Dividend Act is a good idea?

Combined Mentions:

Balanced budget/Spending mentions	37%
Want to get check	18%
Tax mentions	8
Others would benefit, poor, elderly	6%

THE ULTIMATE SELF INTEREST

TABLE 8

Why do you think that the National Profit Sharing
and Dividend Act is a bad idea?

Not workable/Won't work/ Would not help	11%
Government would spend the money/Congress would not stop spending	11
It can't meet the deficit/Would not balance the budget	6
Money should go to federal programs	4
Don't approve of it/Don't agree with it/There is nothing right about it	4
It is ridiculous/It is stupid/ Just a bad idea	4
It will never pass/Congress will never pass it	4
It is socialism/Socialistic government idea	3
Other	53
Total	100%

MARKET OPINION RESEARCH/PETER HART POLL

TABLE 9

Why do you think that the National Profit Sharing
and Dividend Act is a <u>bad</u> idea?

Combined Mentions:

Not workable/Congress would not pass	32%
Would not hold down spending, taxes	22
Give-away, welfare socialism	18
Anti-corporation	10

THE ULTIMATE SELF INTEREST

TABLE 10

[ASKED BEFORE NATIONAL DIVIDEND ACT IS EXPLAINED:]

Suppose that Congress was able to balance the federal budget, say by 1991. In the years after 1991, how likely is Congress to keep the budget balanced?

[ASKED AFTER]:

Do you think a national profit sharing dividend would or would not help keep the federal budget balanced?

Could Congress keep budget balanced?	Total	Would national dividend help?	Total
Very likely	11%	Would	54%
Somewhat likely	28	Would not	36
Not very likely	57		
Don't know/Refused	4	Don't know/Refused	9
Total	100%	Total	100%

MARKET OPINION RESEARCH/PETER HART POLL

TABLE 11

Recently, the U.S. Congress in Washington passed the Gramm-Rudman Act -- how familiar are you with the Gramm-Rudman Act?

	Total	Rep.	Indep.	Dem.
Very familiar	8%	9%	10%	8%
Somewhat familiar	43	48	36	40
Haven't heard	44	40	47	47
Don't know/Refused	4	3	8	4
Total	100%	100%	100%	100%

[IF VERY OR SOMEWHAT FAMILIAR]

Overall, do you favor or oppose the Gramm-Rudman Act?

	Total	Rep.	Indep.	Dem.
Strongly favor	16%	24%	13%	7%
Just somewhat favor	36	42	36	28
Just somewhat oppose	16	13	14	20
Strongly oppose	19	7	22	32
Don't know/Refused	13	13	15	13
Total	100%	100%	100%	100%

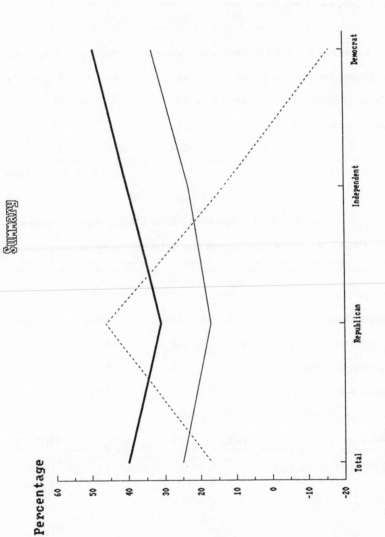

Summary

Percentage

All lines are positive minus negative responses
* Question early in interview
** Question later in interview

MARKET OPINION RESEARCH/PETER HART POLL

Methodology, Questions and Results

The data in this summary are from a telephone study of fifteen hundred (N=1500) adults across the country conducted March 1-12, 1986.

The questionnaire for the study was developed jointly by Market Opinion Research and Peter Hart Research Associates. Attached is a copy of the interview instrument showing the relevant question wordings and sequence of interview. Percentage responses are also given.

Sampling, interviewing and data tabulation were conducted by Market Opinion Research. The geographically stratified, probability - proportionate - to - size sampling frame has 300 sampling points and is based on the adult population of the United States. Telephone numbers are randomly generated by computer for working telephone exchanges; within each household, respondents eighteen years and older are selected using a procedure which yields a proper balance of men, women and age groups. The sample was checked against census data and, where necessary, adjustments weights applied. All telephone interviewing was conducted by Market Opinion Research employees working in Market Opinion Research's Detroit - area interviewing facilities.

The sampling error for a random sample of fifteen hundred is approximately plus or minus three percentage points at the 95% level of confidence.

THE ULTIMATE SELF INTEREST

N=1,500
Dates of Interview:
March 1st thru 12th, 1986

National Dividend Act
Question Results

		T	R	I	D
N1. On another issue — do you think that most American corporations do or do not pay their fair share of federal income taxes?	Do.	23%	27%	20%	20%
	Do not.	72	67	76	76
	Don't know. . .	4	6	4	3
	Refused/NA. . .	*	*	--	*
N2. Suppose corporations paid a top income tax rate of 46% — do you think that would or would not be a fair share for corporations to pay? (N=1079)	Would	53	52	49	56
	Would not . . .	36	37	36	34
	Don't know. . .	11	11	13	10
	Refused/NA. . .	1	1	1	*

N3. Recently, the U.S. Congress in Washington passed the Gramm-Rudman Act — how familiar are you with the Gramm-Rudman Act — very familiar, somewhat familiar, or haven't you heard about the Gramm-Rudman Act?

	T	R	I	D
Very familiar . .	8	9	10	8
Somewhat familiar	43	48	36	40
Haven't heard . .	44	40	47	47
Don't know. . . .	4	3	8	4
Refused/NA. . . .	*	--	--	*

N4. Overall, do you favor or oppose the Gramm-Rudman Act? (WAIT FOR RESPONSE AND ASK:) Would you say you strongly (favor/oppose) or just somewhat (favor/oppose) the Gramm-Rudman Act? (N=773)	Strongly favor. . .	16	24	13	7
	Just somewhat favor	36	42	36	28
	Just somewhat oppose	16	13	14	20
	Strongly oppose . .	19	7	22	32
	Don't know.	13	13	13	13
	Refused/NA.	*	*	2	--

T=Total
R=Those respondents who identify themselves as Republicans.
I=Those respondents who identify themselves as Independents.
D=Those respondents who identify themselves as Democrats.

* Less than .5% mention.

106

Let me read you some proposals which have been made to reduce the federal budget deficit and I'd like to know if you favor or oppose each one. First, do you favor or oppose (READ ITEM)

(READ IN SEQUENCE)	Favor	Oppose	Don't Know	Refused/ NA	PDI[a]
N5. Three year freeze on all <u>increases</u> in federal spending -- that is, no spending increases in any federal programs, including programs such as national defense, Social Security and Medicare.	39%	58%	3%	*%	-19
N6. Let federal spending continue to go up and pay a 5% increase in your federal income taxes.	22	76	2	*	-54

N7. If you had to choose, which would you prefer. . .

		Prefer		
(ROTATE)	T	R	I	D
a. A three year freeze on all <u>increases</u> in federal spending -- that is, no spending increases in any federal programs, including programs such as national defense, Social Security and Medicare.	54%	57%	54%	52%
OR				
b. Let federal spending continue to go up and pay a 5% increase in your federal income taxes.	29	28	21	32
Don't know	*	*	--	--
Refused/NA	17	14	24	17

---

[a]PDI: Percentage Difference Index=% "Favor" minus % "Oppose."

		T	R	I	D
N8. Suppose that Congress <u>was</u> able to balance the federal budget, say by 1991. In the years <u>after</u> 1991, how likely is Congress to <u>keep</u> the budget balanced -- very likely, somewhat likely, or not very likely?	Very likely	11%	13%	9%	11%
	Somewhat likely . .	28	27	25	28
	Not very likely . .	57	56	61	56
	Don't know.	4	4	4	4
	Refused/NA.	*	--	1	1

Now I'd like to explain a proposal called "The National Profit Sharing and Dividend Act." This act is designed to make it easier for Congress to keep the federal budget balanced. There are four main things this act would do. In order to make sure you understand this proposal, let me summarize each of its main points and I'd like you to tell me if each one <u>is</u> or <u>is not</u> clear to you? (AFTER READING EACH ONE, ASK:)   Is that provision generally clear or not clear to you?

(READ IN SEQUENCE)	Clear	Not Clear	Don't Know	Refused/ NA	PDI[a]
N9. (Under this act), all federal income taxes paid on corporation profits would be put in a separate trust fund at the U.S. Treasury each year.	77%	22%	1%	*%	+55
N10. (Under this act), if there is a federal deficit in a given year, this trust fund would be used to pay the difference between what the government takes in and what it spends.	87	11	1	*	+76
N11. (Under the act), any money which was left in the trust fund <u>after</u> paying the budget deficit would be paid out to all adult Americans as a <u>national profit sharing dividend</u>. All American citizens 18 years of age or older would receive a yearly profit sharing dividend check for as much as $900 per person. In years when the federal budget isn't balanced, there would be no money left in the corporate income tax trust fund and there would be no national profit sharing dividend paid that year.	86	13	1	*	+73
N12. Because Americans would want to receive their national profit sharing dividend check, this act would make members of Congress much more reluctant to spend more than the government takes in.	87	12	1	*	+75

[a]PDI: Percentage Difference Index=% "Clear" minus % "Not Clear."

MARKET OPINION RESEARCH/PETER HART POLL

		T	R	I	D
N13. Based on what you understand about the National Profit Sharing and Dividend Act, do you favor or oppose the proposal? (WAIT FOR RESPONSE AND ASK:) Would that be strongly (favor/oppose) or just somewhat (favor/oppose)?	Strongly favor.	22%	21%	20%	24%
	Just somewhat favor . .	34	31	35	37
	Just somewhat oppose. .	14	15	16	13
	Strongly oppose	17	20	15	14
	Don't know.	12	13	14	11
	Refused/NA.	1	1	1	*

N14. What are some of the reasons you (favor/oppose) this proposal? (PROBE FOR AT LEAST TWO RESPONSES -- "What else do you find appealing about this proposal?"/ "What do you think are the problems with this proposal?")

109

THE ULTIMATE SELF INTEREST

Now, I'd like to go over some of the specific provisions of the National Profit Sharing and Dividend Act, and have you tell me if you think each one is a good idea or a bad idea? The first provision is that (READ ITEM) — is that a good idea or a bad idea?

(ASK IN SEQUENCE)	Good Idea	Bad Idea	Don't know	Refused/ NA	PDI[a]
N15. Federal income taxes paid on corporation profits would be put in a trust fund at the U.S. Treasury, and kept separate from income taxes paid by individuals.	62%	27%	10%	1%	+35
N16. In any year there is a federal deficit, money from the corporate trust fund would be used to pay off as much of the deficit as possible.	76	20	4	*	+56
N17. Money left in the trust fund after paying the deficit would be paid out as a national profit sharing dividend.	62	32	5	*	+30
N18. The profit sharing dividend would be paid to all adult American citizens, 18 years or older, who are registered to vote.	56	40	3	*	+16
N19. The national profit sharing dividend would average as much as $900 per person each year.	61	33	6	*	+28
N20. The same national profit sharing dividend would be paid to all adult Americans, regardless of their income level.	53	43	4	*	+10

[a]PDI: Percentage Difference Index=% "Good idea" minus % "Bad idea."

110

Here are some statements others have made about the National Profit Sharing and Dividend Act, and, for each one, please tell me if you agree or disagree with it. First, do you agree or disagree that (READ   STATEMENT)?

(RANDOMIZE Q.21-Q.24)	Agree	Neither Agree Nor Disagree (VOLUNTEERED)	Disagree	Don't know	Refused/ NA	PDI[a]
N21. Instead of paying a national profit sharing dividend, it would be better to let the U.S. government spend the corporate income tax revenues on federal projects and programs.	45%	6%	44%	5%	*	+ 1
N22. Since Americans contribute to the profitability of corporations through their consumer purchases, it makes good sense to let Americans share in those corporate profits.	62	4	31	4	*	+31
N23. The National Profit Sharing and Dividend Act is just another government giveaway program.	36	5	52	7	*	-15
N24. Corporations and business leaders are very likely to oppose the National Profit Sharing and Dividend Act.	78	3	13	5	*	+65
(ASK Q.25 & Q.26 IN SEQUENCE)						
N25. Because Americans would want to receive a national profit sharing dividend check, members of Congress would become much more reluctant to spend more than the government takes in.	63	4	29	5	*	+34
N26. If Congress is ever able to balance the federal budget, a national profit sharing dividend would help keep the federal budget balanced.	61	4	28	7	1	+33

		T	R	I	D
N27. Do you think a national profit sharing dividend would or would not help keep the federal budget balanced?	Would.	54%	52%	47%	59%
	Would not. . . .	36	42	37	31
	Don't know . . .	8	6	15	9
	Refused/NA . . .	1	1	1	1

[a]PDI: Percentage Difference Index=% "Agree" minus % "Disagree."

N28. Based on what you've heard so far about the National Profit Sharing and Dividend Act, would you say that this proposal is a good idea which should be considered by Congress or a bad idea which should not be considered by Congress? (WAIT FOR RESPONSE AND ASK:) Would you say it is a very (good/bad) idea or a fairly (good/bad) idea?

	T	R	I	D
Very good idea. . .	26%	23%	25%	31%
Fairly good idea. .	38	36	36	40
Fairly bad idea . .	9	12	6	8
Very bad idea . . .	14	17	14	12
Don't know.	12	13	20	8
Refused/NA.	*	*	1	1

N29. Why do you think it is a (good/bad) idea? (PROBE FOR AT LEAST TWO RESPONSES)

	T	R	I	D
N30. Suppose a candidate for Congress supported the national profit sharing and dividend act -- would this give you a more favorable or less favorable impression of the candidate? More favorable. . .	52%	49%	40%	59%
No difference . . .	20	19	30	18
Less favorable. . .	19	23	19	16
Don't know.	8	8	10	7
Refused/NA.	1	1	--	*

MM. One proposal to help reduce federal spending is called the line item veto. The line item veto would give the President the authority to decide where to cut spending in bills passed by Congress. Do you favor or oppose giving the President this authority in order to reduce federal spending?

Favor	44%	59%	38%	31%
Oppose.	50	35	54	65
Don't know. . . .	5	6	7	4
Refused/NA. . . .	*	*	--	1

TOWARDS A RESTORATION OF FISCAL

DISCIPLINE IN THE FEDERAL BUDGET:

A RADICAL PROPOSAL

CENTER FOR STUDY OF PUBLIC CHOICE

GEORGE MASON UNIVERSITY

FAIRFAX, VIRGINIA

FEBRUARY 1987

In fiscal year 1986, the federal deficit reached $221 billion—its all time high. Each year since 1970, the federal government has run a deficit. In fact, in 25 of the past 26 years the federal government has spent more than it has collected in revenue. Consequently, the national debt—which gradually fell as a percentage of the GNP following World War II—has in the past six or seven years consistently outpaced economic growth, as it exceeded the staggering level of $2 *trillion* in the past year. In 1964, the interest paid annually on the national debt was $57 per person in constant (1972) dollars. By 1985, this had risen to *$241* in those constant dollars—an increase of over *400%* in real terms despite the fact that the population in 1985 was 20% *larger* than in 1965. The deficit problem is clearly out of control and getting worse.

While all political parties blame the *other* political parties for the growth of the deficit, and politicians constantly point accusing fingers at one another, in fact few if any politicians do not purport to believe that the deficit constitutes a grave danger to the nation and to the economy. The first proposed amendment to the U.S. Constitution designed to mandate a balanced budget was introduced as long ago as 1976. By the summer of 1979, most political pundits in Washington were predicting the imminent passage of a law by Congress mandating a balanced budget. The current administration has strongly promoted a balanced budget amendment, a line-item presidential veto, a capital budget, and other measures intended to eliminate, or at least mitigate, the burgeoning deficits. Numerous plans have been introduced in the Congress designed to accomplish the same end. But in spite of the widespread concern about the problem, and the fact that practically no one is in favor of continuing large deficits, none of these various plans and solutions has actually been enacted. The principal exception is the Gramm-Rudman-Hollings Balanced Budget Act, passed in late 1985, that established a phased deficit reduction plan intended to produce a balanced budget by 1991. Even with this Act in place, the 1987 deficit is expected to top $174 billion, and the prospects of even this relatively modest plan remaining in effect beyond the current Congress are poor.

There are many reasons for this apparent inability of national political leaders to eliminate the deficit problem. Opponents of a constitutional amendment to balance the budget express reservations about tieing the government's hands with an unwieldy and inflexible limit. Critics of the line-item veto argue that such a provision would shift political power from the Congress to the executive branch excessively. Meanwhile, although practically all legislators oppose deficits *per se*, individual legislators typically prefer that someone *else's* constituents bear the brunt of budget-balancing spending cuts or tax increases. Democrats insist that defense spending be cut; Republicans respond that domestic programs should be slashed. As a result, the paradoxical situation has emerged in which almost everyone opposes continuing deficit spending, but no general agreement can be reached on a strategy to eliminate or even meaningfully reduce such deficits.

It is probably extremely unlikely that the Congress will ever succeed in achieving a balanced budget simply by everyone getting together and agreeing to act responsibly. At the same time, there appears to be determined opposition to each of the most widely touted institutional mechanisms designed to help restore a balanced budget. Many of these disputes are ultimately philosophical—e.g., whether there are dangers associated with introducing economic policy into the U.S. Constitution—and seem unlikely to be ever completely resolved. Further, much of the debate tends to become drawn off into side issues; many conservatives want budgets to be balanced at the same time that government spending is reduced, while many liberals fear that balanced budgets will mean excessively stingy government.

Fortunately, there is an alternative which would solve the deficit problem while avoiding most of the sources of political conflict, and also while steering clear of the many and various concerns which have been voiced regarding the different budget balancing reforms. This alternative is also extremely simple. Namely, freeze the federal budget at current levels for a five year period.

This alternative has numerous attractive features. Firstly, it is extremely simple, and simplicity is a major asset in terms of achieving political agreement. Secondly, a budget freeze avoids the allocational issues—i.e., whose ox should be gored—which have stymied virtually all attempts to restore balance to the federal budget over the last decade. *No* programs will be cut, and therefore no significant questions of equity need be raised. Thirdly, a simple budget freeze will have widespread appeal to voters, who public opinion polls consistently show to believe that reducing the deficit is a top national priority. It is a fair way of distributing the burden of balancing the budget that should be very attractive to voters.

How would a freeze work to balance the federal budget? The answer is that it wouldn't—but economic growth would. If the budget simply stopped growing, even without increases in tax rates, federal *revenues* would continue to increase, assuming positive rates of economic growth. As revenue growth outpaced expenditure growth, the deficit would gradually decline; in a short time, the federal government would actually be in *surplus* (a common experience for most of U.S. history, however unusual in recent years).

How short a time would be required before the federal budget was once again in surplus? Surprisingly, even given the huge size of the federal budget deficit, probably in three years, possibly in as little as two. The Congressional Budget Office (CBO) has in recent years been noted for its relatively conservative forecast of economic growth rates and subsequent revenue growth projections. Assume that the level of federal expenditures is frozen at the fiscal year 1988 figure of $1,069 billion. The fiscal year 1988 deficit will be, according to CBO, about $169 billion (note that this is the most recent projection). But the fiscal year 1989 deficit will fall to $107 billion; fiscal year 1990 to $19 billion and by 1991 the federal budget would be in *surplus* by about $69 billion. Assuming a constant rate of growth in federal revenues from fiscal year 1992 to 1993, by 1993 the surplus would reach $244 billion [see TABLE 1].

Some economists prefer to consider the federal deficit from the perspective of the national income and product accounts (NIPA). The NIPA estimates of federal government activity differ from those of the budget in several ways, mostly involving the timing of transactions and the treatment of financial activities. Financial transactions which only involve the exchange of existing assets and liabilities are assumed to be "paper transactions" and, in general, are excluded from the NIPA, because they generate no current income

---

TABLE 1
THE EFFECT OF A BUDGETARY FREEZE AT FY 1988 LEVELS ON THE SIZE OF THE FEDERAL DEFICIT:
Budgetary Aggregates

[all figures in billions of dollars]

	1988	1989	1990	1991	1992	1993
Total Revenues	900	962	1050	1138	1220	1313
Total Expenditures	1069	1069	1069	1069	1069	1069
Size of Deficit	-169	-107	-19	+69	+151	+244
Deficit as % of Total Outlays	-15.8	-10.1	-1.7	+6.5	+14.1	+22.8

Source: Congressional Budget Office, The Economic and Budget Outlook: Fiscal Years 1988-1992 (Congress of the United States, 1987); and additional calculations. Revenue projections for 1993 assume the same growth rate for the previous year.

or output. For example, the sale of an asset of the federal government—e.g., Conrail—would reduce the budget deficit but have no effect on the NIPA deficit. Direct lending by federal agencies like the Small Business Administration is included in the budget but excluded from NIPA. Normally, the differences between the two alternative measures are relatively small. Still, these "relatively small" differences can amount to many billions of dollars, so it is worth considering the outcome of a budget freeze in terms of the NIPA as well.

Again assume that a budget freeze is declared at fiscal year 1988 levels. In terms of NIPA expenditures, this amounts to $1,111 billion. The fiscal year 1988 NIPA deficit will be about $158 billion. As a result of the freeze, this would decline to $89 billion in fiscal year 1989, and become a *surplus* of $7 billion in fiscal year 1990. By fiscal year 1993, assuming a constant rate of growth of federal revenue from the preceding fiscal year, the NIPA federal sector would be in surplus by $275 billion [see TABLE 2].

In short, employing CBO's traditionally relatively pessimistic revenue forecasts, the federal budget would be substantially in surplus within three fiscal years of the implementation of a budget freeze, according to both of the major ways of calculating the size of the federal deficit. In fact, according to the method of deficit calculation most preferred by economists, within two years of a budget freeze the federal deficit would be entirely eliminated, and the budget in *surplus* equalling about .6% of federal outlays.

Perhaps most importantly, a budget freeze would show voters once and for all that the deficit problem is *not* an insoluble dilemma, somehow beyond the abilities of real government and mortal politicians. Voters have been told so long by politicians in both major parties that the deficit was an immensely complex problem whose resolution was no less difficult than, say, learning to control the weather, that many have understandably acquiesced to ever-growing deficits. But of course, deficits are not like hurricanes and

118

politicians are not analogous to weathermen. The deficit problem can be resolved as simply as it arose. One of the drawbacks of many of the proposed budget-balancing reforms (e.g., the balanced budget amendment, or the line-item veto) is that the mechanism by which they are supposed to work is not easy to understand. Some would even argue that such reforms wouldn't work at all. By contrast, a budget freeze is at once a simple plan and one which would obviously and *necessarily* work. The absence of various political bells-and-whistles might cool the ardor of some current proponents of certain reforms, but at the same time increases the

---

TABLE 2
THE EFFECT OF A BUDGETARY FREEZE
AT FY 1988 LEVELS ON THE SIZE OF THE
FEDERAL DEFICIT:
National Income and Product Account

[all figures in billions of dollars]

	1988	1989	1990	1991	1992	1993
Total Revenues	953	1022	1118	1206	1293	1386
Total Expenditures	1111	1111	1111	1111	1111	1111
Size of Deficit	-158	-89	+7	+95	+182	+275
Deficit as % of Total Outlays	-14.2	-8.0	+.6	+8.5	+16.3	+24.7

Source: Congressional Budget Office, The Economic and Budget Outlook: Fiscal Years 1988-1992 (Congress of the United States, 1987); and additional calculations. Revenue projections for 1993 assume the same growth rate for the previous year.

likelihood that it would actually leave the drawing board and be implemented. Once voters understand that the deficit problem *can* be solved, the probability of large deficits ever emerging again in the federal budget will be radically reduced.

TESTIMONY OF

JOHN H. PERRY, JR.

To The

HOUSE WAYS AND MEANS COMMITTEE

John H. Perry, Jr. was invited to testify before the Ways and Means Committee of the U.S. House of Representatives on July 25, 1985. The transcript of his appearance follows:

STATEMENT OF JOHN H. PERRY, JR., CHAIRMAN, AMERICANS FOR THE NATIONAL DIVIDEND ACT, INC., ACCOMPANIED BY GEN. WILLIAM C. WESTMORELAND, U.S.A. (RETIRED)

Mr. PERRY. Thank you, Mr. Chairman.

My name is John H. Perry, Jr. I am the chairman of the Americans for the National Dividend Act which is now currently before the Ways and Means Committee, H.R. 56, and we thank you for this opportunity to testify because we feel that this is a pivotal issue before the Congress at the moment, considering the enormous increases in the deficits in the last few years, and while this general classification has been labeled discussion of the President's tax reform we feel that this act does have many provisions in it which will simplify the Internal Revenue Code besides which its main purpose is to rid the Federal Government of any further deficits.

This period of time required for this is approximately 4 years. There are nine of the Ways and Means Committee members as co-sponsors of this act, and they have been very helpful in helping to redefine it and define it.

But I think the first mission I have here is to describe what it is.

THE ULTIMATE SELF INTEREST

H.R. 56 contains five basic provisions. The central innovation of the plan, and it is described over on these displays over there, is the creation of a national dividend trust fund in which all Federal corporate income tax receipts would be placed instead of being spent as part of the Government budget. The fund would be distributed to all registered voters so long as the Federal deficit did not exceed the amount of the trust.

Dividend payments would increase as corporate profit increased. In order to discourage budget deficits the total funds available for the national dividend would be reduced each year by any Federal budget deficit.

This provision gives voters a vested self-interest reason for resisting Federal deficits. In other words, they will insist to their Congressman that instead of spending beyond our means that they spend within our means so that he can receive a share of the corporate income tax collections which will have to be out of the budget surplus.

The third provision is the elimination of double taxation of dividends. This would end Federal personal income taxes on corporate dividends and would attract investment dollars into the private sector thus creating new jobs and stimulating economic growth.

This particular provision of H.R. 56 would eliminate between 50 and 300 provisions of the Internal Revenue Act and would simplify the Tax Code tremendously.

The fourth provision is a cap on the Federal corporate tax rates. At its present level of 46 percent, it would be up to the Congress to determine what the percentages are, in no way attempts to tell the Congress how much to tax, it merely sets a parameter so that business can make business decisions and plan its future.

And, five, this would be phased in over a 5-year period to prevent disruption of existing Federal programs. During this time a moratorium would be placed on new Federal spending programs.

In other words, this freezes Federal expenditures for 5 years. At the end of the fourth year, using the OMB figures, you get into surplus out of which you can then start paying the national dividend to all registered voters.

Now, in order to illustrate how this would work, if you look at the colored chart on the right there, this has been brought up to date so that if you were to enact the law this year and freeze Federal expenditures at the end of the fourth year, the Federal Government would be in surplus.

Now it seems to me this is the critical thing before the Congress today. You have had efforts at line item vetoes, which apparently is not getting anywhere, the President's tax proposal is worrying about tax fairness and as your Chairman Rostenkowski says that is not the problem, the problem is getting the Federal budget under control.

I know it is in this morning's paper that the interest charges for the first 9 months of this fiscal year hit $139.6 billion; that is the one charge you can't eliminate except over time by reducing deficits and debt.

Since this problem seems to get bigger every year, we have been trying to find a fundamental solution and we think we have found this in these five provisions so that you have the following benefits.

I have listed those in the center chart there, there are six of them. There are others, but the main ones are as follows: In the first place, this is an income redistribution process so nobody can really argue that you are not helping people in the lower income brackets.

This is a progressive plan. The second thing it does, and most of the Congressmen, all of the Congressmen I have ever talked to agree that they will not dare to vote for a deficit if this plan were in effect because they would be taking money out of their constitutent's pocketbooks. I have researched this over the years and they all agree on that.

Third, it doesn't require any tax increases. By freezing Federal expenditures and using that as your parameter when you are making up your budget you get an opportunity to let your growth revenues increase—then at the end of the fourth year, surpass the expenditure level, and then rapidly the surpluses increase so that you then could either cut taxes or whatever the Congress would decide to do.

The beauty of this whole plan from an economist's standpoint is that it stimulates the economy with earnings instead of deficits.

Keynesians' philosophy has been around for years and to some extent it has worked very well. They have stimulated economies out of deficits but we now have such an enormous debt structure and deficit that we have to find a better way to do this. We feel H.R. 56 is the vehicle to do it. You stimulate the economy out of earnings instead of deficits and this is extremely important in our opinion in the current slowdown in the economy because unless something is done to turn that slowdown around, we may get into budget deficits that are irreversible.

Finally, and the beauty of the whole plan is this: It encourages the producers to work for the benefit of us all. That concludes my summary of the statement. I would be glad to take and field any questions.

[The prepared statement follows:]

STATEMENT OF JOHN H. PERRY, JR., CHAIRMAN, AMERICANS FOR THE NATIONAL DIVIDEND ACT

Mr. Chairman thank you for this opportunity to testify before your Committee on H.R. 56, the National Dividend Act of 1985. H.R. 56 is a proposal that I and others have worked on for many years. We believe that it is an idea whose time has come. The bill has an impressive bi-partisan group of co-sponsors.

I believe that our runaway federal deficits are the most serious threat facing our nation. Next year our total debt will approach $2 trillion dollars. Interest alone on our debt will be close to $135 billion this year. And interest on the debt is rising faster than any other item in the budget. In short, we face a national crisis of alarming proportions. Something new and dramatic must be done in order to avert what most certainly will become a national disaster.

A solution, I believe, must be politically feasible in order to succeed. It must treat each and every citizen fairly and impartially. And finally, it must clearly recognize that we can't continue to spend money that we haven't first earned.

H.R. 56, I believe, will do those things.

    (1) It will redistribute income;

    (2) It would end federal deficits;

    (3) It will not require tax increases;

    (4) It does not cut social programs;

    (5) It will encourage the producers to work for the benefit of us all.

H.R. 56 is not a new proposition. Over the last decade, this plan has been studied and scrutinized in every detail by intelligent people including prominent economic

THE ULTIMATE SELF INTEREST

leaders and universities. And its credibility as a common-sense solution to the potential disaster confronting our nation has grown steadily.

Mr. Chairman, I would like to summarize the elements of the National Dividend Act at this time. I have provided for the record more detailed information including a copy of the bill, H.R. 56.

CREATING A CONSTITUENCY FOR REAL ECONOMIC GROWTH

The National Dividend Plan is a comprehensive economic proposal to revitalize the most powerful economic machine in history—the American Economy—and to allow all of our citizens to participate and benefit from this success. The plan accomplishes this by instituting five related reforms that will encourage participation in the private sector and assure a federal budget surplus.

Those five reforms are the heart of the National Dividend Act, H.R. 56, now pending before Congress.

I. National profit sharing

The central innovation of the Plan is the creation of the National Dividend Trust Fund. All federal corporate income tax collections would be deposited in this Trust. Instead of being spent as part of the government budget, the fund would be distributed in annual dividends to all registered voters. Dividend payments would increase as corporate profitable productivity increased.

Funds would be distributed through local banks using local voter registration lists. Banks would be compensated for the expenses involved by serving as interest-free depositories for specified short periods of time.

While the dividend payments would be exempt from federal taxes, they could be subject to state and local taxes (at the discretion of state and local governments). This additional revenue could enable states and cities to operate with no new taxes.

Because only registered voters would receive dividend payments, the Plan would increase participation in the voting process.

II. Discouraging budget deficits

Total funds available for the National Dividend would be reduced each year by any federal budget deficit. This feature is called the Automatic Dividend Deduction (ADD). The ADD provision of the National Dividend Plan gives every voter a vested, self-interest reason for resisting federal deficits. A federal deficit would become a major political liability to a member of Congress, because that member would be held directly responsible for the reduction or absence of his constituents' dividend checks.

III. Eliminate double taxation of dividends

Corporate profits presently are taxed twice by the federal government, first at the corporate level and again on the individual level when distributed to shareholders as dividends. Such a tax creates a disincentive to invest.

The National Dividend Pay would end federal personal income tax on corporate dividends. This would attract investment dollars into the private sector, thus creating new jobs and stimulating economic growth.

IV. A cap on corporate tax rates

The National Dividend Plan addresses the issue of placing a ceiling on the federal corporate income tax rate. The plan is flexible on the level at which the cap would be established. However, it suggests that the rate should not exceed 46 percent, the current rate.

V. Control Government Expansion: pay as we earn

The National Dividend Plan would be phased in over a five year period. To prevent disruption of existing federal programs during this time, a moratorium would be placed on new federal spending programs. The moratorium would permit revenues, increasing from normal economic growth, to catch up with current spending levels without threatening existing government services.

In the first year, one-fifth of all corporate income taxes would be paid into the Trust Fund. In the second year, two-fifths, and so on. In the fifth year the program would be fully operational.

The Plan requires no new taxes and would be funded entirely by earned dollars, as opposed to tax or deficit dollars. No additional layer of bureaucracy would be required to administer the Plan, since all money would be distributed through private banks.

Most important of all, the National Dividend Plan would guarantee a majority constituency against excessive government spending and reward productivity of the American people.

The NDP is a recognition of the fact that this country's economic problems are not caused by flaws in the science of economics. They are the unquestionable result of our political system which weighs the impact of competing interest groups in its decision-making process. H.R. 56 will direct this process away from the "special interest" and toward the general interest.

We believe the National Dividend Plan is unique in that it will treat the entire electorate in the same unbiased way. It will provide the incentive for the electorate to permit Congress to take the necessary (and unprecedented) steps to cap spending until revenues catch up.

Mr. Chairman, I have recently written a book, "The Ultimate Self-Interest," in which I have attempted to explain this proposal in language that the average taxpayer can understand. Many who have read it have indicated that, indeed, they do understand it and they want to see it become law.

I submit the "Ultimate Self-Interest" as part of this testimony.[1]

Mr. Chairman, each day that we delay passage of H.R. 56 it costs the taxpayer ½ billion dollars in Federal deficits.

Thank you for the opportunity to appear.

---

[1] The book "The Ultimate Self-Interest: Keeping Our Country Solvent" has been retained in the Committee files.

I. National Profit Sharing

The central innovation of the Plan is the creation of the National Dividend Trust Fund. All federal corporate income tax collections would be placed in this Trust. Instead of being spent as part of the government budget, the fund would be distributed in quarterly dividends to all registered voters — so long as the federal deficit did not exceed the amount in the Trust. Dividend payments would increase as corporate productivity increased.

II. Discouraging Budget Deficits

Total funds available for the National Dividend would be reduced each year by any federal budget deficit. This feature is called the Automatic Dividend Deduction (ADD). The ADD provision of the National Dividend Plan gives every voter a vested, self-interest reason for resisting federal deficits.

III. Eliminate Double Taxation of Dividends

The National Dividend Plan would end federal personal income tax on corporate dividends. This would attract investment dollars into the private sector, thus creating new jobs and stimulating economic growth.

IV. A Cap On Corporate Tax Rates

The National Dividend Plan addresses the issue of placing a ceiling on the federal corporate income tax rate. The plan is flexible on the level at which the cap would be established. However, it suggests that the rate should not exceed 46 percent, the current rate.

V. Control Government Expansion

The National Dividend Plan would be phased in over a five-year period. To prevent disruption of existing federal programs during this time, a moratorium would be placed on new federal spending programs. The moratorium would permit revenues, increasing from normal economic growth, to catch up with current spending levels without threatening existing government services.

1. IT REDISTRIBUTES INCOME.

2. IT WOULD END FEDERAL DEFICITS.

3. IT DOESN'T REQUIRE TAX INCREASES.

4. IT DOESN'T CUT SOCIAL PROGRAMS.

5. IT STIMULATES THE ECONOMY WITH EARNINGS INSTEAD OF DEFICITS.

6. IT ENCOURAGES THE PRODUCERS TO WORK FOR THE BENEFIT OF US ALL.

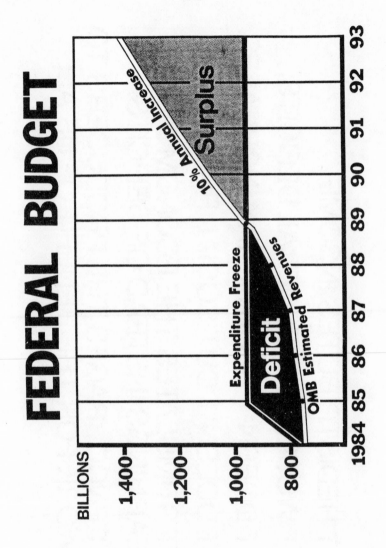

Fri., May 31, 1985   ST. LOUIS POST-DISPATCH

commentary

$800 A Year For Every Registered Voter

National Dividend Plan Would Balance Budget, Reward Citizens With Cash

By Wyche Fowler And Henson Moore

For the past two years, the most pressing domestic problem has been our huge federal budget deficit. As Congress continues to struggle with the issue, most of the suggested solutions depend on the traditional answers to budget problems — reduce spending, increase taxes or apply some combination of the two.

But history has shown us that cuts in spending run into hard-to-resist pressures of special interest groups and that tax increases only go toward further spending. Even the across-the-board spending freeze that some talk about would not address the problem permanently. What is needed is a program that will give the voters a sufficient incentive to ensure that they will use their power, their votes, to reward those who work for a balanced budget and to punish those who don't.

We have recently co-sponsored legislation that we believe will provide this needed new approach for the results we are all seeking. It is an interesting proposal, and, more importantly, it is a workable plan not only to bring about a balanced budget but to actually create a surplus in federal budgeting. The program is called the National Dividend Plan and we are convinced that not only can it achieve the results we need in reducing the federal deficit, but it can make extremely beneficial contributions to our economy in other ways. The dividend plan does not deal with taxes and raising money; Congress can decide to raise revenues the way it wants.

Instead, NDP is complementary; it works on the spending side through a form of national profit-sharing, and to us it constitutes a realistic formula for solving the most pressing economic problem facing us.

The National Dividend Plan has five interrelated provisions:

▶ All federal corporate income tax collections would be put into a national profit-sharing trust fund that would be distributed annually on a per capita basis to all U.S. registered voters. Based on last year's figures, this formula would have put approximately $800 in the hands of each of some 127 million Amer-

icans. This payment would not be subject to federal income tax. As a result, voters would look for more corporate profits rather than less and would soon have a much better understanding and develop better support for the effective functioning of our marketplace economy.

▶ In order to put an end to further federal deficits and to halt the rise in the federal debt, there would be no national dividend payments unless there was a surplus. This would bring pressures on Congress to achieve such a goal.

▶ In order to ensure that there is a surplus as quickly as possible, there would be a five-year, across-the-board

freeze on federal spending. Analysis shows that revenue growth would put us in surplus in two to three years. A moratorium on federal expenditures has already been proposed by many and has received significant support.

▶ In order to ensure that there would be maximum incentive for profitable productivity, the present double tax on dividends would be eliminated. Shareholders would receive their dividends free of federal income tax. This would have many beneficial effects in improving business efficiency, eliminate about 300 sections and subsections of the present tax code and enable businessmen to start making business decisions instead of tax decisions.

▶ In order to ensure that the temptation to push federal corporate taxes be-

yond the point of diminishing returns is resisted, there would be a ceiling at the present 46 percent maximum rate. This would ensure maximum revenue for both the registered voter and the corporate stockholder whose ownership rights would be greatly strengthened.

In terms of the federal budget deficit, the key element in the National Dividend Plan, of course, lies in the provision for reducing the amount of the deficit. Realistically, a balanced condition in federal operations would take as much as five years to achieve, although there is a ground for hope that it could come sooner, but there would be no payments to citizens until then.

We believe that the 127 million registered American taxpayers would embrace the prospect of receiving a payment of almost $800 a year from the government; that embracement would be so strong that the pressure to balance the federal budget — and maintain that balance — would assure the elimination of deficit spending.

It would be a brave congressman and a brave administration that would be prepared to face constituents with an explanation that dividends to voters are impossible because there are pressing needs of the government this year that outrun revenues. In short order, we would find excessive government expenditures melting away, unnecessary programs brought under control, expenditures and revenues bearing a close relationship to each other — all because the voters would insist on such results out of their self-interest in obtaining their national dividend.

As deficits continue to add up, it becomes increasingly important to recognize that procrastination in effectively dealing with overspending is not only the worst option we can select, but the most dangerous economically. And, above all, it is something our country simply can no longer afford.

Wyche Fowler is a Democratic representative from Georgia and Henson Moore is a Republican representative from Louisiana. Both of them are members of the House Ways and Means Committee.

Wednesday, October 5, 1977   Philadelphia Daily News   *

By Chuck Stone

NDP Would Pay $750 Dividend for Your Vote

It's possible that John H. Perry Jr., a 60-car-old millionaire, and I are on different ides of the fence of economic ideology.

But we share a common civic obsession. We both want to maximize the largest number of votes in federal elections.

President Carter's proposed Universal Voting Registration Act is one legislative strategy for supporting that civic concern. Under the act, American citizens could register to vote on a federal election day.

To paraphrase the song, walk right in, sit right down, and baby, let your vote hang out.

PROOF THAT ELECTION Day registration significantly increases voter turnout are Minnesota, Wisconsin and Maine. In the 1976 Presidential election, Minnesota led the nation with a 72 percent voter turnout. Wisconsin and Maine were fourth and fifth, respectively.

In 1977, no alibi can justify nonvoting. Any American's refusal to vote defaults on his or her civic rent, and anybody who doesn't pay civic rent ought to be evicted from democracy's house. (I warned you it was one of my obsessions.)

While I scold in frustration at such electoral apathy, Perry, a successful president of several companies and an acknowledged leader in the development of commercial submarines and ocean habitats, has authored an ingenious electoral support program called the National Dividend Plan.

NDP would actually pay you to vote in federal elections.

Over a five-year span, NDP would be phased in gradually until a maximum of $750 per voter is reached.

CONCEIVABLY, A FAMILY of five voters would receive cash benefits of $3,750 almost enough to pay an average yearly college tuition for three students.

NDP takes cognizance of a fundamental human trait that has governed all human behavior since the earliest efforts to devise a harmonious society.

"Feed men, and then ask of them the virtue," wrote Dostoyevsky.

"It is an unfortunate human failing," President Franklin D. Roosevelt once declared in a speech, "that a full pocketbook often groans more loudly than an empty stomach."

In different ways, both men were suggesting the identical equation: Electoral involvement increases in direct proportion to economic self-sufficiency.

PRACTICALLY EVERY study of voting patterns shows a high correlation between socio-economic status and voter turnout. Poor folks just don't see any reason to vote.

While NDP seeks to increase voter participation, it actually has a larger agenda: a national profit-sharing plan that would change the corporate tax structure and restrict government spending, especially in social welfare programs.

This last July 1, Perry testified before the Senate Subcommittee on Taxation and Debt Management.

He summarized NDP as a four-step process:

1.) Corporate and shareholder taxes would be integrated into a single tax not to exceed 50 percent, thus doing away with the "double tax" on stock dividends.

2.) Corporate tax revenues would be paid directly into a National Dividend Trust Fund and distributed quarterly as a dividend to the voting public on a per capita basis.

3.) A moratorium on any new federal expenditures would go into effect while the National Dividend was being phased in over the five-year period.

4.) "When fully effective," testified Perry, "the National Dividend would be reduced in relation to the amount of the federal deficit so that only the 'profit' net of any increase in the deficit would be available for distribution to the public."

Ay, there's the rub.

A **LARGE FEDERAL** budget deficit would reduce proportionately NDP's payment to voters. It's possible that if somehow spending got out of hand, voters would receive nothing.

What Perry anticipates is that enlightened voters with a vested interest in protecting their $750 would put restraints on a spend-thrift Congress and profligate President. Theoretically, that works. But 24.3 million

Americans who live below the poverty line and are deprived of minimally decent housing, health care and nutrition still need some form of expanded government assistance.

In Perry's booklet, "Perspective," he objectively assesses "the liberal phenomenon" and "the conservative reaction" within the context of what liberals have tried to do (and failed in many areas) and why conservatives, in the light of historical experience respond with documentable apprehension.

So many well-intended liberal programs have not only proved to be extravagant ripoffs of the poor but have submerged the federal budget in an ocean of deficit from which it has yet to recover.

What has been ignored, Perry argues persuasively, is that "national economic progress may not have been due to the inherent role of government, but instead to the inherent strength and productivity of American business. In short, success has come not because of, but in spite of governmental intervention."

NDP'S BRILLIANTLY conceived "economic restructuring" may or may not be immediately implementable, given existing federal budgetary commitments.

But a national dialogue on NDP is in democracy's best interests.

Moreover, anybody who is anxious to multiply the number of American voters is my kind of person. Especially if he's a millionaire.

Columnist Pete Dexter is ill.

130

THE CINCINNATI ENQUIRER   JANUARY 22, 1984

A Quick Solution To Budget Deficits

BY THOMAS GEPHARDT
Associate Editor of The Enquirer

HOW WOULD YOU feel about a single congressional enactment that accomplished *all* of the following objectives?

• Abolish federal budget deficits and halt the growth of the federal debt.

• Impose a five-year ban on the growth of federal spending.

• Encourage individual investment and savings.

• Generate wider understanding and support of the free-enterprise system.

• Increase productivity in American business and industry, making the United States more competitive with such economic powers as Japan and West Germany.

• Encourage business to make its investments for business reasons, not for tax reasons.

• Increase voter registration and, in all probability, voting.

• End the taxing (actually, the double-taxing) of dividends.

• *And* distribute a national dividend of between $700 and $1,000 to every registered voter every year.

ALL OF these goals, say supporters, would follow as night the day enactment of the National Dividend Act of 1984.

The idea of a national dividend sprang some 20 years ago from the mind of Florida newspaper publisher and oceanographer John H. Perry Jr. In the past two decades, he has submitted it to economists, accountants and members of Congress, inviting their suggestions and incorporating many of them into plan revisions. Now he has enlisted several dozen members of Congress — Democrats and Republics, liberals and conservatives, blacks and whites — as sponsors.

"It hit me," Perry explains, "that if we could divert part of the earnings of corporations directly to the electorate, it would have a tendency to cut off demagogic appeals to the vote getters — or buyers."

Perry proposes, specifically, that all the income taxes paid by U.S. corporations — between $80 billion and $100 billion yearly — be put into a trust fund. The federal deficit would have the first claim on the trust fund. But any excess would be distributed among America's registered voters.

THE IDEA is to give every American a vested interest in seeing to it that (1) federal spending does not get out of hand and (2) the federal budget is balanced. Dividend-hungry Americans, Perry believes, would outweigh in influence with Congress all the special interests that today are importuning Congress for subsidies, grants and exemptions.

What Congress would hear, as a result, would not be a few voices demanding *more* spending, but millions of voices demanding *less*. What Congress would see would be less indifference to budget deficits and more clamoring for a balanced budget. Only when the budget was balanced, after all, would the whole national dividend trust fund be available for distribution to registered voters.

One haunting question is whether those who derive a major share of their income from the federal government would co-operate. Would their interest in getting their share of the national dividend override their obvious stake in a continuation of high government spending?

YOU CAN'T help thinking of the private employers who thought they could make their employees more company-minded by giving them stock in the company. The idea was to see that every employee had a personal stake in larger company profits, translatable into larger dividends for his stock. In many cases, however, it has turned out that most employees prefer higher take-home pay today to larger dividends tomorrow — particularly when it's the pay rather than the dividends that puts bread on the table.

Perry argues that no acceptable alternative has come to light in the 20 years since he advanced the idea of a national dividend. Instead, he says, the urgency has become all the more important — what with staggering deficits that Congress and even a conservative President seem incapable of harnessing.

When that point is reached, say supporters of the national dividend, it's time to change our way of doing business.

THE NATIONAL DIVIDEND plan is more complex than the idea of a balanced-budget amendment, which is inching its way to national consideration. Yet it holds the hope of achieving far more widely shared goals.

The question is whether it can enlist enough congressional attention to generate a real debate. It is to attract that attention that an organization known as Americans for the National Dividend Act Inc. has been formed, with headquarters at 1901 N. Fort Myer Drive, Rosslyn, Va. 22209.

131

THE ULTIMATE SELF INTEREST

7177

B4—The Sacramento Union, Sunday, February 26, 1984

EDITORIAL PAGE

The Sacramento Union
Founded March 19, 1851

Richard M. Scaife
Publisher

Barry Hopwood
President

Peter J. Hayes	Robert H. Badgley
Vice President and Editor	Vice President & General Manager
Daniel J. Sabol	Richard T. McGrath
Managing Editor	Marketing Director

Offices at 301 Capitol Mall, Box 2711, Sacramento 95812 Phone 442-7811

Plan to curb deficit

Conservative politicians for years have been seeking a way to reverse the slide towards bankruptcy caused by government's propensity to spend indiscriminately.

As deficits continue to mount, this would be a good time for Congress to seriously consider a revolutionary plan to refinance the country devised years ago by industrialist John Perry.

Perry's National Dividend Plan calls for a new sort of revenue sharing under which federal taxes collected on earnings of corporations would be diverted directly to the pockets of voters.

The idea is that if politicians never got their hands on the funds, they could not squander them to buy votes by funding special interest programs.

Distributing the funds that corporations pay in federal income taxes to registered voters on a per-capita basis also would give citizens a vested interest in the health of the nation's economy.

It also would underscore the fact that money comes from the private sector, not from government.

The National Dividend Plan would impose a moratorium on federal budget increases and set the maxium rate of the federal corporate income tax at the present 46 percent.

Corporate income taxes would be placed in a profit-sharing trust fund to be divided among voters.

A key provision is that the amount paid to voters from the trust fund would be reduced when there was a federal budget deficit.

This presumably would increase public pressure to eliminate deficits.

Proponents of the plan estimate that it would give consumers $80 billion to $100 billion, increasing purchasing power and providing a stable demand for the production of goods.

If the thinking of the plan's proponents is sound, it would save money by lifting many low-income people above the welfare threshold. And many high-income voters would invest their dividends in stocks and bonds, which would further boost the economy.

There might be serious flaws in the National Dividend Plan.

But, as AP business analyst John Cunniff said, "some profound economic minds have studied the concept and have become converts."

132

The Patriot-News Co.

HARRISBURG, PA.   Edwin F. Russell   AUGUST 2, 1984

Raymond L. Gover   **PRESIDENT**   Henry H. Young

PUBLISHER   EXECUTIVE EDITOR

A Free Press — Armor of the Republic

Capitalism for everybody

UPON INITIAL inspection, Florida businessman John H. Perry's National Dividend Plan appears to be just another dressed-up "spread-the-wealth" scheme of the type populists have been promoting for years.

But as envisioned by Perry and endorsed by conservative economist Milton Friedman, the five-point plan may be the "magic bullet" for erasing the national deficit. In this respect, it hardly could do worse than any of the other arcane economic formulae issuing these days from the government and financial communities.

Basically a carrot-and-stick approach, the plan proposes per-capita distribution of corporate income tax receipts, a dividend based on surplus, a five-year freeze on federal spending, elimination of the double tax on dividends, and a ceiling on the corporate rate fixed at the present 46 percent maximum level. Perry calls it capitalism for everybody, and sees it as incentive for everything from voter registration to reduced unemployment.

THE LOGIC is irresistible, and presents our lawmakers with a plausible structure for a truly "popular" economy. The only problem is that to perform as it should, the dividend plan must be taken whole-cloth, something Congress in its deliberative magnificence is not likely to do. The absence or alteration of just one of its components would throw the plan into such imbalance that Washington would find getting out of the plan probably twice as difficult as getting into it.

National Dividend Plan Is Plugged In Area

By Sally Bixby Defty
Of the Post-Dispatch Staff

Imagine that in 1989 the federal deficit — now estimated at about $200 billion annually — has vanished.

Imagine that each registered voter is getting $1,000 a year, tax free, and will continue to so long as Congress passes no budget that makes the deficit grow again.

Imagine that if the voter invests that $1,000, the dividends it earns would be tax free, as will dividends be he receives from any other sources.

Too good to be true? No, says Florida businessman John H. Perry, who has been committed to the idea of what he calls the National Dividend Plan for more than 20 years.

Along the way, his concept has been the subject of seminars at the prestigious Conference Board, and the Harvard School of Business, which Perry attended after graduating from Yale.

His idea has won enthusiastic approval from some distinguished economists and businessmen — and from members of Congress as disparate as liberal Rep. Parren Mitchell, D-Maryland, and conservative Rep. Newt Gingrich, R-Ga. Former Senate Majority Leader Howard H. Baker of Tennessee says the proposed legislation has "a great deal of merit."

The plan was praised in two 1975 radio broadcasts by the man who is now president, Ronald Reagan.

Perry was in St. Louis to lobby for his plan and to promote his newly published book on the topic, "The Ultimate Self Interest: Keeping Our Country Solvent."

There are five basic components to the bill that will be introduced in Congress for a second time in January and that would establish the National Dividend Plan. They are:

— Congress must freeze spending for a period of five years.

— A National Dividend Trust Fund would be established, with all corporate tax revenues going into it in increments of 20 percent each year until at the end of the five-year period all corporate taxes would go into the trust fund.

— The present maximum corporate tax rate, 46 percent, would be frozen for five years, encouraging investor confidence and business investment. Perry would like to subsequently see it drop, to about 40 percent, for the same reason.

— The so-called double tax on dividends would be eliminated. Corporations pay taxes, and then dividends to shareholders; at present the shareholders pay taxes on the dividends. Perry's plan would exempt from personal income tax all dividends, both those from stock ownership and from the National Dividend Trust Fund.

— After the budget deficit is eliminated, through the National Dividend Trust Fund, the fund would then pay each registered voter an annual dividend.

"This year corporate tax collections will be close to $100 billion," Perry said, "and there are about 100 million registered voters. That would be an annual dividend of $1,000 per registered voter, or $2,000 for a husband and wife."

By the end of the five year period, Perry says, the deficit would be gone.

Moreover, the nation's registered voters would be so delighted to be getting as much as $1,000 paid to them quarterly that two things would happen, Perry says. The voters would pepper their elected representatives with demands that no further deficits be incurred, because the deficits that could cut or eliminate their dividend.

Perry also says the attitude toward business would change. It would be difficult for a worker to see an as an adversary the employer whose profits bring him a quarterly check.

"Lots of corporations pay no taxes at present because they are not making a profit," Perry said. "I think the public would be very cooperative in trying to make them more profitable by cutting regulations and red tape, by buying American."

Perry says the dividends would require no new bureaucracy for their distribution. "The government would just send out 51 checks, to each state and the District of Columbia, based on the number of registered voters there. Within each state, banks would

John H. Perry
Reagan praised his plan

disburse the funds for the privilege of having free use of the money for, say, 90 days. Signatures on voter registration forms could be used to prevent fraud."

Dividends for those who have died or do not pick them up would go back into the trust fund.

But how does the federal government make up for the revenue lost through diversion of corporate taxes to the trust fund? How does it make up for the lost revenue on dividends?

Perry says corporate taxes in 1964 were 26 percent of federal revenue, while today they make up only 8 percent. Because corporate taxes would be phased in, 20 percent a year, that would mean an annual loss of only 2 percent. And because federal revenues historically have grown at about 10 percent annually, thus — Perry says — removal of the corporate profit tax collections would still result in a revenue gain of about 8 percent a year.

Perry is 67 and lives in Palm Beach, where he hads three corporations that deal in cable television and oceanographic businesses.

ST. LOUIS POST-DISPATCHER · 11/22/84

WAYS AND MEANS COMMITTEE

7180

DON YOUNG CONGRESSMAN FOR ALL ALASKA

FOR IMMEDIATE RELEASE
May 2, 1985

YOUNG CO-SPONSORS NATIONAL DIVIDEND ACT

WASHINGTON - Rep. Don Young (R-Alaska) is a co-sponsor of legislation that if enacted would create a national dividend plan for registered voters, once the Federal budget has been brought into balance.

The National Dividend Act, HR 56, has five basic provisions:

1. A National Dividend Trust Fund would be set up. All federal corporate income tax collections would be placed in this trust fund. These funds would be held in trust for all legally registered United States, voters and would be distributed on a quarterly, per capita basis to those voters. The dividends would be exempt from federal taxes.

2. To ensure that there would be no further federal budget deficits, a registered voter would, in effect, be paying for any deficit because he or she would not get the full national pro rata dividend unless the government first earned a surplus.

.3. Double taxation on corporate dividends would be eliminated.

4. Maximum corporate tax rates would be frozen at the current 46 percent level.

5. A five year spending freeze would be imposed on the federal budget.

"This plan represents a bold, new idea in addressing the federal budget deficit crisis," Rep. Young said. "It provides a grass roots incentive to reduce spending and bring our budget into balance. A balanced budget would reduce the pressure on interest rates and inflation, and the additional capital generated by the dividend plan would be a boost to our economy, providing jobs and increasing business expansion," he added.

-30-

Mr. GEPHARDT. Thank you, Mr. Perry, for your statement. Questions? Mr. Schulze.

Mr. SCHULZE. Thank you, Mr. Chairman.

Thank you, Mr. Perry. It is an intriguing proposal. What would happen to interest rates were this proposal enacted?

Mr. PERRY. We feel interest rates would definitely come down. I have written several pamphlets on it and studied it with many economists and the reason why is because you are putting into the economic structure both supply side and demand side economics and you are getting as a result a stable economy.

You see, you had supply siders come along and put emphasis on supply side and it did some good but it hasn't solved the problem and prior to that you had the Keynesian demand side economists and that is what got us on the wrong track to start with.

We took on more programs than we could afford. This way all the voters are going to get behind this plan because their dividends are going to come out of earnings from a stable economy.

Mr. SCHULZE. Why use corporate taxes? Why use general revenues?

Mr. PERRY. You can't use any other type. The corporate revenues are a different type of tax. It is the only tax that does not add expense. The profit is the difference between cost and value, and any other kind of tax like a value-added tax and so forth just adds to the cost. You only make a profit if you cut your costs below what you can sell your product or service for.

Mr. SCHULZE. Doesn't this then infringe on the rights of the corporate owners or the stockholders?

Mr. PERRY. No, this reinforces the rights of the stockholders because you are getting rid of the tax on dividends and the public will recognize the value of the producer, he is producing for all of us.

He still has the incentive to make a profit but he is making a profit for the benefit of everybody, whereas the way it is today, that profit that goes into the corporate income tax is merely going into the general fund and many times is being used against him.

Mr. SCHULZE. What effect then would it have on unemployment?

Mr. PERRY. I think it would do more than anything else to reduce unemployment. For instance, you would never have another movement to keep raising the minimum tax because that would cut down your profits.

Mr. SCHULZE. I guess my next question is to General Westmoreland.

General, in your opinion, can we afford a defense spending freeze? Would that be beneficial?

General WESTMORELAND. It depends upon the level at which you freeze it. With the budget now before the Congress, I believe we will properly take care of defense and if it is frozen at that level over a period of 5 years that would be I think welcomed by the Department of Defense and it would give them something to program on.

One of the things that has plagued the Department of Defense over the years is their difficulty in long-range programming because they cannot depend upon any particular level of defense funding over a period of time.

Mr. SCHULZE. Thank you, General.

Your background as a military man is well known. How did you get involved with this? Can you tell me your relationship with this program?

General WESTMORELAND. Well, I am, I believe, a responsible citizen. I devoted approximately 40 years of my life to serving the U.S. Government and the people. I have been retired now from the military for 13 years. I became acquainted with John Perry. As a responsible citizen, I have been concerned about the problems with our economy and the instability involved with the interest rates and deficits.

I am very cognizant of the fact that for the first time in our history I believe Federal deficits have become a political problem and when I met with John and he and I talked for hours and hours, I have attempted to analyze the plan, and I have concluded that it is a sound concept, and it is the only plan that I am aware of that takes care of the fundamental problem as explained, I think, in a very articulate fashion by John Perry.

Mr. SCHULZE. Thank you, General.

Thank you, Mr. Chairman.

Mr. GEPHARDT. Mr. Fowler.

Mr. FOWLER. Mr. Chairman, thank you.

As a cosponsor of the national dividend plan, I want to welcome Mr. Perry and commend him for his public citizenship.

As many know, Mr. Perry is a very distinguished private citizen, entrepreneur, and a very fine thinker, who has devoted a considerable amount of his resources to developing this plan over the years, asking nothing in return, and for that and that alone—on this day of think tanks and everybody with all the rabbits running different ways, trying to solve our Nation's deficit and budgetary problems— I want to commend him for the work that he has put into this.

It is a plan, it seems to me, that is comprehensive, that has a vision of how to discourage deficits in the future, how to get out of the $220 billion deficit that we are in, how to control Government expansion and is certainly compatible with the President's program to cap corporate rates.

I would like to ask Mr. Perry to elaborate on your theory that I think is unique to this plan of how to get this money.

What is it in this plan that enables us to pay our way out by earnings rather than deficits? Specifically, how does that work?

Mr. PERRY. Well, as you know, the plan provides that distribution to the registered voters comes from the corporate income tax collections at the Federal level.

This has no bearing on what the States wish to do with their own rates of corporate taxes but at least when you cap the Federal Governments, you are preventing it from taxing beyond the point of diminishing returns. The States can compete with each other and that is a good thing, because otherwise there will be no limit to how much they could tax their own citizens.

But the purpose of the plan is to really get the producers, the entrepreneurs and the stockholders, to work on behalf of society as a whole rather than being condemned for earning a profit and then having the money they pay over to the Federal Government go into some waste bucket as I call it.

137

I am not saying that all Government expenditures are a waste, but I do say that there have been lots of studies made by the Grace Commission which show enormous amounts of waste.

I think if this plan were put into effect much of that would disappear because everybody would be very cost conscious knowing it would have a significant effect on their future.

Mr. FOWLER. What about in the short term—while we are holding a lot of people at present benefit levels? There are those who are concerned that, particularly low-income people would be hurt by this transition in the program from deficits to profits before they would begin to benefit. How would you deal with that?

Mr. PERRY. I am glad you asked that question, and it is certainly a legitimate concern. I haven't had the chance to do a detailed analysis of it but have done a lot of thinking on it with my associates. We feel certain there is a method by which that short-term problem could be overcome by having the Treasury advance moneys that would normally not be paid out until such times as the national dividend equaled or surpassed the current COLA income.

Mr. FOWLER. You mean borrowing from future surpluses?

Mr. PERRY. Yes; because if you look at the chart there as soon as you get the thing under control and can have the national dividend as the quid pro quo for freezing expenditures, you get the country in very good shape and you are administering funds that you can't beat as far as efficiency is concerned.

One of the studies we had done in the 1970's, it was the Lionel Edie Co., showed that in the case of New York State, which they analyzed, it showed that the percentage of efficiency by distributing the money directly to the voter was almost 100 percent, whereas the present method at the time to distribute the welfare, the cost of overhead was 56 percent.

So over half of your dollar is paid out in administrative costs, and the company, which was the Lionel Edie Co., when I first had the study done, they said they would not endorse it, but when they got all through they said this is so good we do endorse it.

Mr. FOWLER. Have you had a chance to analyze the President's tax reform proposal as to its revenue neutrality? In your opinion, is it revenue neutral or does it lose money?

Mr. PERRY. I think it is going to lose money. I am basing that on what other people have studied about it.

Mr. FOWLER. Thank you very much, Mr. Chairman.

My time is up.

Mr. GEPHARDT. Mr. Duncan.

Mr. DUNCAN. Thank you, Mr. Chairman.

I would also like to welcome Mr. Perry and General Westmoreland to the committee.

Have you ever discussed this plan with the administration or prior administrations in the White House?

Mr. PERRY. Yes, sir, I have had several discussions with President Reagan when he was Governor. In fact, he came to see me one time or we arranged to meet because his chief mentor at the time was a Congressman named H.R. Gross. H.R. Gross, when he retired from the Congress, made his total farewell address on the national dividend plan. We had a very good meeting. When he got in to be

138

President, his supply siders got hold of him and I got shunted aside, but I think it is going to turn around now.

Mr. DUNCAN. How many years have you been working on the plan?

Mr. PERRY. Actually 20 years.

Mr. DUNCAN. Have you discussed it with a President other than President Reagan?

Mr. PERRY. I have had some of the best brains in the country develop this with me, ex-Assistant Secretaries of the Treasury, former Treasurers, economists, and many Members of Congress. It is something we have developed over this period.

Mr. DUNCAN. Have you had other people assisting, consulting and working with you on the plan——

Mr. PERRY. Yes. My particular contribution happens to be just the initial idea of taking the corporate taxes, but Assistant Secretary of the Treasury Ernie Christian, for example, was the one who developed the idea of not paying it out until you earn it.

I have had an economist who suggested the freeze back in the midsixties. Features like that have come from other people.

Mr. DUNCAN. How would States and cities benefit from the plan?

Mr. PERRY. They would get in revenue through the growth revenues of the national dividend plan an amount that would exceed, according to the last figures we had on it, what they were formerly getting from revenue sharing.

Mr. DUNCAN. Thank you very much, and thank you, Mr. Chairman.

Mr. GEPHARDT. Mr. Rangel.

Mr. RANGEL. Thank you very much, Mr. Perry and, General, it is always a pleasure for us to see you. I just want to state for the record that I am surprised that your legislation hasn't really moved faster in front of this committee than it has, and especially in view of the fact that we have the chief deputy whip supporting it, Mr. Martin, who is the Governor of North Carolina; Mr. Vander Jagt, who is an outstanding leader in the Nation; Mr. Moore, who is running for Senator; Mr. Flippo; Mr. Nelson; Mr. Hance; Mr. Jenkins; Mr. Shuster; Mr. Hefner; Mr. Anthony; Mr. Ford; Mr. Gray; Mr. Spence; Mr. Duncan; Mr. Quillen; Mr. Jones; Mr. Roemer; Mr. Mitchell; Mr. Campbell; Mr. Young; Mr. Downey; Mr. Bonior; Mr. Crane; Mr. Montgomery; Mr. Darden; Mr. Rowland; Mr. Hartnett; and Mr. Dorgan.

You have done an outstanding job convincing Members of Congress, and more particularly, members of this committee as to the merits of this legislation.

What do you think really prevents this from getting the hearing which its sponsors obviously think it deserves?

Mr. PERRY. We are in the hearing, so nothing. Everything has its time in life. We feel the time is now. While I get discouraged, I realize that we have made quite a bit of progress, but I certainly appreciate your comments.

Mr. RANGEL. I am glad that you have not lost your optimism and I would like to also thank you as the chairman of the Select Committee on Narcotics for not being one of these Americans who just talk about how dangerous it is to the Nation, but for your outstanding effort in making sure that some of these people who violate international and national law are brought to justice.

I am amazed how one individual can be so active in so many areas and at the same time be optimistic that we can turn this country's economy around as well as address our drug trafficking problem. You are a great credit to this Nation.

Mr. PERRY. Thank you.

Mr. RANGEL. Thank you, Mr. Chairman.

Mr. GEPHARDT. Mr. Vander Jagt.

Mr. VANDER JAGT. Thank you very much, Mr. Chairman.

I would like to associate myself with the remarks that the gentleman from New York just made and the earlier remarks of Mr. Fowler. I think the committee is honored by the presence of our witnesses.

General Westmoreland, you have appeared before congressional committees many times over the years. I suspect this is the first time you have ever appeared before the tax-writing committee and we welcome you to Ways and Means.

Mr. Perry, you have had a fantastic success in business and in the scientific, technological, and publishing fields, and much of your success has come through your innovative and creative ideas. It is nice to see that you have turned that creativity and innovation to economic and political thinking. I guess I admire most your persistence and dedication to this idea. I think it is probably 20 years and God only knows how many resources you have expended to bring this to the attention of the public and to the Congress, and there is nothing in it for you except a better America, of which you are a citizen. I commend you for your efforts.

But as Mr. Rangel read that list of sponsors, it as astounding to me how you span the political spectrum. You have conservatives on it, you have liberals on it, you have Republicans on it, you have Democrats on it, and at first blush, the plan sounds a little bit socialistic in that you are having the Government distribute cash to every individual not on the basis of anything they have done or produced. It sounds a bit like McGovern's plan, mail out a $1,000 to every citizen.

Doesn't it have a socialistic twinge to it?

Mr. PERRY. It is the opposite because it cuts out the Federal Government's distribution of that money. It goes directly to the citizens and doesn't rely on some bureaucratic organization to decide who gets how much. That is why it is so efficient. Everybody gets the same and it encourages everybody to take a greater interest in their government.

Mr. VANDER JAGT. One of the things that intrigues me about the plan is you would be creating a constituency for holding down spending. Right now we have a collection of special interests all of whom want increased spending, but the desire of the public in general for lower spending is so thin so the benefit is not directly felt in the pocketbook of an American citizen.

This really would create a nationwide constituency for the Government holding down its spending, wouldn't it?

Mr. PERRY. Yes. This would give the Congressmen a good excuse to say no.

Mr. VANDER JAGT. Another thing that has intrigued me as I have watched the plan over the years is it has been refined, it has changed, as Mr. Duncan brought out, in his thinking because of the input of so many different experts that you have called upon. I wonder—this is really a difficult question to answer, but we were talking about this plan 12 years ago. If it had been adopted back then, what do you think the state of the economy would be today?

Mr. PERRY. Well, I think the plan 12 years ago was imperfect, and it wasn't until 1977, when Ernie Christian and myself attended the Harvard Business School and one of the students asked us what made me think this would stop deficits and I did not have an answer. Ernie Christian went home that night to Washington and found the answer and that is what he calls statutory ratcheting. You don't pay out the dividend until you have a surplus.

I considered in retrospect that the plan was not totally foolproof until that day. Then I saw a dozen Senators and Congressmen. The first person I saw was Bob Packwood and I told him about the change in the plan and he said, "You have found an answer to the Federal deficits," and ever since then, every Congressman has said the same thing.

Mr. VANDER JAGT. Thank you.

Thank you, Mr. Chairman.

Mr. GEPHARDT. Mr. Heftel.

Mr. HEFTEL. Thank you, Mr. Chairman.

It is good to see you again, Mr. Perry and, General Westmoreland. I suppose it is unfortunate that now President Reagan was more impressed with Mr. Laffer's curve than he was with your proposal because if we have a problem with deficits, it was born of this administration and I think it makes it much more difficult for any system to solve the problem because you are dealing in virtually a $2 trillion deficit, a $200 billion a year deficit. How long does it take you before you eliminate that $2 trillion deficit in terms of being able to redistribute the profit, if you will?

Mr. PERRY. In the first place, it isn't a $2 trillion deficit. It is a $2 trillion debt and the first move is to get the deficit under control and if you get the deficit under control and you have a growing economy, the debt really isn't too important and also if you keep your interest rates down.

Mr. HEFTEL. Do you think that you have to retire that $2 trillion deficit?

Mr. PERRY. No, you don't. In fact, it may not be a good idea. The main problem now is to get the deficit under control so you can restore confidence and keep stimulating the economy so the Government doesn't wake up one day and find revenues far shorter than they thought they were going to be.

Mr. HEFTEL. It is interesting that Ernie Christian made a major contribution to your program. He also made a major contribution, I think it was called safe harbor leasing. It is interesting some of the things that come from downtown Washington, but in any event, I hope that somehow in the passage of time that we in the Congress can control deficit spending whether it is your mechanism or not, I don't know, but if we don't have a mechanism, then we are in very serious trouble because until we are capable of telling the electorate we can't spend money we haven't got, we are headed for higher deficits and a total higher debt structure.

Mr. PERRY. Thank you.

I think the first step is the recognition by all of you people that there is a problem and that you have to do something about it pretty soon.

Mr. HEFTEL. Thank you and thank you, Mr. Chairman.

Mr. GEPHARDT. Mr. Moore.

Mr. MOORE. Thank you, Mr. Chairman.

I can't resist a comment on the comment made by the gentleman from Hawaii, a good friend. I can't accept for a moment the fact that all the deficits in this country were born in this administration. I don't believe anybody believes or accepts that. I am sure he misspoke with that comment.

We are glad to have both of you here. This bill, this idea, is proof to me that the best ideas in this country don't come from Government, but come in fact from the private sector and very creative people. This is a very creative, novel, radical idea and that may be why it has taken so long to catch on, but I think it is catching on.

Could you capsulize for a moment what is the driving motivation behind this bill of yours working and being successful? Why will it work?

Mr. PERRY. It will work because everybody, whether because he is a registered voter or because he is a consumer, will feel a greater interest in his country. For example, if you were an automobile purchaser to be, and you went out to buy a car, you would think twice about buying a foreign car because by buying a foreign car, you would not be promoting your own self-interest. That is the reason for my book, "The Ultimate Self-Interest," to try to show that it is the getting together of our society that is important.

Mr. MOORE. I agree. What I see in this, too, is the fact that you are educating the public and giving them an incentive. It appears to me that all of our efforts we are doing to try to hold down spending don't involve those things, there isn't an incentive for the public to support what we are doing. It makes it frustrating and difficult for us to try to hold down spending, in my opinion unsuccessfully. I think that you are touching upon something that is missing from all the other ideas or efforts we are making to control spending. You are educating the people, giving them their own personal interest in our success and creating an incentive. Something I think about, I think you are probably making every American a capitalist. That might be a very helpful thing.

Mr. PERRY. Yes; that is what it would do, make every American a capitalist, and something far more important, I think it is a possibility of opening up a dialog with the East, because if you were to confront the Russians with this, they would no longer have an argument against capitalism. You would pull the rug right out from under them without firing a shot.

Mr. MOORE. I want to compliment the two of you—the General, for devoting his considerable talents and abilities to again serving his country, and you, for devoting your considerable talents and abilities in the private sector to now serving the country with an idea like this.

I am hopeful that Congress, before it ends, will find the daring to try something that will work. We don't seem to be too successful with the ways we have been trying so far to control spending.

I compliment you.

Mr. PERRY. Thank you.

Mr. GEPHARDT. Mr. Pease.

Mr. PEASE. Thank you, Mr. Chairman.

I would like to make a couple of comments and then maybe ask a couple of questions.

My colleague from Hawaii—I don't know whether Mr. Heftel said that all the fault of the deficits fall on this administration or not. If he did, he did misspeak. I think maybe half have been the fault of this administration, but certainly not all.

I have been happy with the dialog earlier today and in this panel to reassure ourselves that this plan is not Socialist. When I saw the income redistribution angle of it, I was fearful that it might be. But I should have been reassured when I saw Mr. Vander Jagt and Mr. Moore as sponsors, that they would not be associated with anything socialistic.

In your verbal testimony, you referred several times to Keynesian economics. I am not familiar with that term. Could you help me out on that.

Mr. PERRY. Lord Keynes was the prime thinker in using deficits to stimulate the economy back in the 1930's, and actually Roosevelt used that. And it has been used many times in many countries, because if a President, or whatever his title is, gets in a position—for instance, the Argentine—the economy goes sour, the first thing he does is try to figure out a way to stimulate it.

And in many cases, especially in the Argentine this has been true. In fact, Roosevelt stimulated it with military spending because it took the minds of the people off the real problem. In a sense, we are doing that to some extent now.

Mr. PEASE. You mean Lord Keynes?

Mr. PERRY. I mispronounced it, yes.

Mr. PEASE. Let me say this. You propose to freeze Federal spending for 5 years, is that correct?

Mr. PERRY. That is what the act has in it.

Mr. PEASE. That means there would be no cost of living increases for Social Security for a 5-year period?

Mr. PERRY. This allows the Congress to determine whether any specific program can go up or down, but as long as the total does not exceed the previous year.

In other words, it doesn't take any of the prerogatives of the Congress; they still decide who gets how much, but the total has to be fixed.

Mr. PEASE. Have you given any thought as to how we might achieve this freeze for 5 years, whether we ought to omit COLA's or pay the COLA's and cut someplace else?

Mr. PERRY. I mentioned earlier there is a way to solve this problem. I have not had the chance to do the homework on it. As a matter of fact, I hope this committee would do it.

But there is a way to borrow from the future as long as you know that the future is going to have the money.

Mr. PEASE. That wouldn't be a freeze, though.

143

Mr. PERRY. This needs a lot of research. I am just expounding the principle that you could.

The reason I am doing this is because many times when I talk to people about it, they complain I could never get that over because it would freeze the COLA's.

What I am saying is the Treasury could advance x billion dollars—I don't know the exact number, but it would be far less than the total national dividend payment, which is running now around $100 billion—a little less than that at the moment, but it has been up to $100 billion. That is distributed among the entire electorate.

But in order to take care of the problem of the COLA requirements for the elderly or whoever is in need of it, you could borrow a certain amount from the Treasury to be repaid. That could be done by supplementary legislation.

Mr. PEASE. The problem is that under our budgeting system, if we borrow money from the Treasury, that shows up as an outlay in the year that it is made.

Mr. PERRY. You would have to legislate that, that wouldn't be the case.

Mr. PEASE. We would just legislate that borrowing does not constitute borrowing and not affect the freeze. That would be an innovative way to do it.

General Westmoreland, have you checked with Caspar Weinberger on his notions of freezing defense spending for 5 years at the current level?

General WESTMORELAND. I have not talked to him. I think he would welcome some sort of assurance that the defense expenditures, if set at a base that was acceptable, could be continued for a period of 5 years and he would have some assurance that that would be the case.

That would certainly simplify programming in the Department of Defense based on my experience. I have not talked to the Secretary of Defense about this.

Mr. PEASE. It seems to me that is a wonderful suggestion. If we could pick up only that portion of your plan, we could make great progress on the deficit over the next few years.

What would you do, Mr. Perry, about rising interest costs? We can't freeze interest payments; we have to pay those as they come along.

Mr. PERRY. If you have a good, balanced economy and your supply and demand is properly adjusted—in other words, if you let the supply and demand seek its own way—you will find that this would reduce interest rates.

Mr. PEASE. It would not reduce interest payments by the Federal Government.

Mr. PERRY. You can't reduce the ones that are already fixed, but in future borrowings, you could get the borrowing for less.

That has been one of the good side effects of the supply siders. In other words, that is not a totally adequate solution, but it has been a beneficial effect because your interest rates have come way down.

Mr. PEASE. Thank you, Mr. Chairman.

I thank the witnesses. This is certainly one of the more imaginative proposals that has come before the committee.

Thank you.

Mr. GEPHARDT. Mr. Crane.

Mr. CRANE. Thank you, Mr. Chairman.

I want to congratulate two dedicated patriots out here who have distinguished themselves in differing lines of activity, but are nonetheless distinguished in their combined efforts to try and promote the general welfare.

I think that Mr. Perry has put his finger on the source of the problem by recognizing that it is we here in the Congress who control the destiny of this country in the sense that the taxing functions, the spending functions are functions of the Congress, and, in fact, more specifically, of the House of Representatives, inasmuch as all general appropriation bills have always originated here and taxes must originate here, and if you have got taxes and spending, you have it all.

We set the agenda and originate the policy, and thus your effort at trying to build incentives into the system for Congress to respond to constituents in a responsible way is at least the only original kind of idea long those lines that I have seen.

I have no questions. I just wanted to congratulate you for your long-term devoted commitment to this, Mr. Perry, and to congratulate General Westmoreland, whom I had the pleasure of meeting in Taiwan in 1970, and to salute two great patriots and two great Americans.

Mr. PERRY. Thank you.

Mr. GEPHARDT. Are there further questions?

Ms. Kennelly.

Mrs. KENNELLY. Mr. Perry, I am a former secretary of state, and I salute you for the fact that you do recognize the people that vote.

Given the fact that you put so much time into the deficit problem, what do you think about our efforts here on this committee to pass the President's tax reform package from the prospect of the deficit? Are we going to help or hurt it, or will it have no impact?

Mr. PERRY. Brief studies I have seen indicate that you will probably come out with revenue loss.

Mrs. KENNELLY. Do you have any comments about where the shortfall comes from?

Mr. PERRY. In the first place, I don't think it is possible to pinpoint it because you don't have an idea at the present time what the economy will be down the road a year from now.

It doesn't look to me like there is a chance of it going through at least until 1986, and you don't know what shape the economy will be in till then.

Mrs. KENNELLY. But right now, it looks like a revenue loss?

Mr. PERRY. All that I have read on the subject indicates there will be a slight loss of $15 or $20 billion, but I don't put much faith in the figures. Look at what they predicted as deficits 5 years ago.

Mrs. KENNELLY. That is what we are looking at.

Thank you.

Mr. GEPHARDT. Mr. Daub.

Mr. DAUB. Thank you, Mr. Chairman.

I enjoyed very much listening, learning more this way than reading sometimes about your idea.

When you look at the rate of increase in Federal spending from 1977 to 1981, the rate of growth in that curve of actual expenditures was 16 plus 16 plus 16 plus 17, 65 percent. Corporations didn't improve their bottom line 65 percent; Americans didn't get a pay raise of 65 percent during those 4 years. And then we commenced to turn around that rate of growth in Federal spending.

In 1982, we dropped it to 12 and then we dropped it to 8, and the third year to about 5 or 6 percent, but because the numbers in the base are growing at such an alarming rate even though we cut back on the percentage of increase, we continue to produce these not arithmetic but astronomical add-ons to our deficit.

So it seems to me that within a function of a freeze with the priority of the Congress, at least that part of your idea, reassessing which programs within that freeze we raise or lower, is at least an element of sensibility that, if you will note, has been a part of the debate, and not whether or not to cut but, in fact, simplify how much to cut and how to get that done.

So you keep doing what you are doing. We appreciate your contribution. Your ideas, I think, are being more thoughtfully received in the Congress than ever before.

Mr. PERRY. Thank you.

Mr. GEPHARDT. Are there other members who wish to question?

If not, we deeply appreciate your patience and your time being here. Your testimony has been very valuable to the committee, and we appreciate your coming here today.

The committee will be in recess until 2 p.m. this afternoon.

[Whereupon, at 12:05 p.m., the committee recessed, to reconvene at 2 p.m.]

SUMMARY OF NDP

The National Dividend Plan would:

1. Provide for placing all corporate profit taxes collected by the federal government into a National Dividend Trust Fund, which then would be distributed quarterly through private banks to all registered voters on an equal, federal tax free basis.

2. Stipulate that the Trust Fund would be reduced by the amount of any federal budget deficit. Any move by government to resort to deficit spending would run into heavy opposition from voters whose dividends might be reduced or imperiled.

3. Eliminate the federal government's personal income tax on corporate dividends.

4. Retain the 34 percent ceiling on federal corporate income taxes.

5. Declare a moratorium on new, federal expenditure programs throughout the five-year phase-in period.

"Enhanced real growth and reduced inflation emerge as the chief outcomes of applying the provisions of the National Dividend Plan."—Economic impacts of the National Dividend Plan, Merrill Lynch Economics, Inc., 1980

H. R. 2740 is a bill introduced in Ways and Means that represents a total systems approach to our socio-political economic problems.

Passage of the bill would provide a form of national profit sharing, a budget surplus and a mechanism for supply and demand economics to work in harmony.

NATIONAL DIVIDEND ACT COSPONSORS

The following current and former Members of Congress have cosponsored National Dividend Act Legislation:

Bill Alexander	(D-AR)	Ed Jenkins	(D-GA)
Beryl Anthony	(D-AR)	Tom Lewis	(R-FL)
William Boner	(D-TN)	Walter Jones	(D-NC)
Carrol Campbell	(R-SC)	Jim Martin	(R-NC)
Dan Crane	(R-IN)	Parren Mitchell	(D-MD)
Phil Crane	(R-IL)	R.V. Montgomery	(D-MS)
George Darden	(D-GA)	Henson Moore	(R-LA)
Byron Dorgan	(D-ND)	Bill Nelson	(D-FL)
Wayne Dowdy	(D-MS)	Jim Quillen	(R-TN)
John Duncan	(R-TN)	Buddy Roemer	(D-LA)
Harold Ford	(D-TN)	Roy Rowland	(D-GA)
Ronnie Flippo	(D-AL)	Dick Schulze	(R-PA)
Wyche Fowler	(D-GA)	Bud Shuster	(R-PA)
Bill Gray	(D-PA)	Floyd Spence	(R-SC)
Newt Gingrich	(R-GA)	Arlan Stangeland	(R-MN)
Kent Hance	(D-TX)	Bob Stump	(R-AZ)
Thomas Hartnett	(R-SC)	Guy Vander Jagt	(R-MI)
Bill Hefner	(D-NC)	Don Young	(R-AK)
Carroll Hubbard	(D-KY)		

WRITE YOUR REPRESENTATIVES

(ON YOUR LETTERHEAD OR STATIONERY)

Dear Congressman (Senator)...

I have recently read an in-depth report on the purpose and benefits of H. R. 2740, known as the NATIONAL DIVIDEND ACT OF 1987.

I am very interested in its success. I would appreciate you keeping me informed of its progress. I also want to take this opportunity to tell you that I am available to help in the district in any way I can to build local support for this legislation.

I would appreciate knowing your interest in and position on this legislation.

I look forward to hearing from you.

Sincerely,

Your name and title

For further information call or write:

David W. Henderson

Americans for the National Dividend Act, Inc.

1901 North Ft. Myer Drive

Twelfth Floor

Rosslyn, Virginia 22209

(703) 841-0626

EPILOGUE

If the National Dividend Plan had been in effect during the last 10 years, the per capita debt burden of all Americans — every man, woman and child — would be $7,500 less than it is today.

How? The gross federal debt has grown from $773 billion at the close of fiscal 1978 to an estimated $2.6 trillion at the end of fiscal 1988. That's an increased burden over $1.8 trillion placed on an estimated 240 million Americans. This amounts to a $7,500 increase for every American or a $30,000 increase for a family of four. This cost will be borne by a decrease in American living standards.

Think about that and what the impact will be in another 10 years if we don't act now.

J. H. P., Jr.
September 1987

JOHN H. PERRY, JR.

Riviera Beach, Florida

John H. Perry, Jr., is Chairman of two Florida corporations headquartered in Riviera Beach, Florida: Perry Oceanographics, Inc. and Perry Offshore, Inc. The latter is the largest commercial builder of robot and manned submarines in the U.S. Mr. Perry is Chairman of the Perry Foundation, Inc., a not-for-profit corporation.

Mr. Perry is the former President and Chairman of Perry Publications, Inc. which until 1969, operated 28 newspapers in Florida; All-Florida Magazine, a Sunday supplement; Palm Beach Life Magazine; the statewide All-Florida News Service, and numerous commercial printing plants in Florida. Perry Publications pioneered the development of computerized printing of newspapers in the early 1960's. He is a Director of the Nassau Guardian (1844) Limited, Nassau, Bahamas.

From 1966 to 1968, he was a member of President Johnson's U.S. Commission on Marine Sciences, Engineering and Resources which, after two years of study, submitted its report entitled, "Our Nation and the Sea". He served as Chairman of the Commission's technology panel. As President of the Bahamas Undersea Research Foundation, Mr. Perry facilitates marine research at the Caribbean Marine Research Center. Through the Perry Energy Systems Division of Perry Oceanographics, he has developed an energy process for making methanol from sea water.

Mr. Perry was born in Seattle, Washington, January 2, 1917; was graduated from Hotchkiss in 1935, Yale in 1939 and attended the Harvard School of Business Administration.